* * * * * * * * * * * * * * * * * * * *

AN ALTERNATIVE FUTURE FOR AMERICA'S THIRD CENTURY

* * * * * * * * * * * * * * * * * * * *

AN ALTERNATIVE FUTURE FOR AMERICA'S THIRD CENTURY

ROBERT THEOBALD

THE SWALLOW PRESS INC.
CHICAGO

Printed in the United States of America

First Edition
First Printing 1976

Published by
The Swallow Press Incorporated
811 W. Junior Terrace
Chicago, Illinois 60613

This book is printed on recycled paper

Library of Congress Catalog Card Number 75-39845
ISBN-0-8040-0725-X

Contents

Preface 9

PART I: Positive and Negative Scenarios

1 Entering the Eighties: A Time for Despair 17
2 The Impact of the Seventies: Reasons for Hope 28

PART II: Problems and Possibilities

3 Communication Realities and the Conservative Revolution 45
4 Environmental Agreements 53
5 The Temporary Becomes Permanent 56
6 Citizen Participation or Fascism? 65
7 The Impact of Violence 72
8 The Shrinking Northeast 79
9 The Second Corpernican Revolution 85
10 Guaranteed Income vs. Guaranteed Jobs 110
11 Income Distribution and Social Change 125
12 The Potential of the Bicentennial 131
13 Creating Myth for the Communications Era 143
14 Past, Present and Future 150
15 Creating the Future 161

PART III: Individual and Group Action

16 A Call to Celebration 173
17 Jonah / Irene Orgel 179
18 How to Dialogue 188
19 Community Involvement 196
20 North Dakota and the Bicentennial 204

PART IV: Questions, Questions, Questions

21 Questions, Questions, Questions 222

PART V: Futures Conditional 235

PART VI: Feedback 237

To:

The readers of *Futures Conditional* whose feedback enabled much of the writing in these pages.

Preface

This is the third book in a series with similar titles. The first and second editions in 1968 and 1970 were published under the titles *An Alternative Future for America* and *An Alternative Future for America II*. They drew attention to the direction in which we were moving and the dangers we confronted if we did not succeed in changing our patterns of behavior. These editions were based on the assumption that most people were not yet aware that things were already going seriously wrong and were likely to get rapidly worse.

This edition is being completed in June 1975. Those who have kept up with socioeconomic and political trends are now aware that what seemed to be impossible nightmares are coming true. The dystopias [negative Utopias] of writers such as Orwell, Huxley, Vonnegut, and others, are developing rapidly. We appear to be powerless, as a society, to prevent the continuance of destructive trends.

Now that people have become aware of our growing failures, it is no longer useful to concentrate on the negative by showing that our present system is not viable. Our worsening situation is apparent to all those who are willing to look at reality instead of ignoring it. Our need today is to learn how to operate beyond the fear of breakdown and the growing despair which is necessarily generated by an understanding of the realities of our situation.

It is certainly true that the danger of breakdown is very great. It is also true, however, that collapse becomes almost certain if those of us who are most aware of the danger become paralyzed by fear of disaster. While nobody can prove that personkind will survive, the only way to have any chance of developing more hopeful directions is for all of us to strive together to eliminate present dangers and to create present possibilities.

This book is written "beyond despair" in the full recognition that we may not reach the potentials which do exist. However, if we should fail to build a better society, it will be due to a failure of nerve and drive rather than the impossibility of dealing with our problems. I personally have no doubt that personkind has not yet begun to develop its full potential.

In this connection, it is useful to look at the question of whether one should be an optimist or a pessimist at this time. In reality, the question is meaningless because these terms imply that there is a world which exists apart from the actions we take. Thus, while it is true that negative trends do presently predominate, directions can be changed by energy and courage.

An Alternative Future for America's Third Century is therefore designed to challenge citizens to become involved in creating a more human future for America's third century. This volume shares the inspiration of the previous two editions which were produced by Noel McInnis and his students at Kendall College: It is argued that people can, if they are willing, create the future they desire and that this future can be more desirable than that which is presently developing.

There are six parts to this book, each of which has a different style and purpose. Part I suggests the two very different directions which American society may take, depending on our decisions over coming years. The negative scenario shows that our continuing concentration on economic growth, at a time when it is no longer possible, can easily bring down American and Western society. The positive scenario suggests the ways in which we could alter our thinking and beliefs and, thus, not only deal with our immediate policy crises but also create a more human society. In order to make the scenarios more vivid, they are reported as if they were summaries of the experience of the seventies.

Part II enlarges on some of the themes which are suggested by these scenarios. It examines the fundamental changes in thinking which are necessary and suggests the new directions which will be required in dealing with education, income distribution, work, etc. These materials state, in effect, the extraordinary a-historical challenge that we now face.

Part III provides materials designed to inform and encourage anybody who wants to learn how to act effectively to influence the direction of his/her community. It provides a variety of action and thought possibilities which can open up new directions for those who are concerned with creating a more human future.

Part IV consists of questions which were asked by students at Maryville College in Maryville, Tennessee in connection with a convocation conducted by me there in March, 1975. They suggest the extraordinary range of issues opened by the shift from the industrial era to the communications era.

Part V provides information about how you can obtain additional resources and learn about opportunities for involvement in case you believe you can be involved in the movement to create America's Third Century.

Part VI gives examples of some of the feedback which I received following a pre-publication edition of this book.

This book is based on the assumption that a growing number of people are engaged in an increasingly conscious process of creating a more human society. It is written in the hope that you, the reader, are one of them, and that you will want to link with others in this common purpose.

Robert Theobald
Summer, 1975

PART I: Positive and Negative Scenarios

The two scenarios which follow cannot possibly come true. They are not designed to predict history but rather to set up self-denying and self-fulfilling prophecies.

This book is written on the assumption that decisions by individuals affect the direction of the overall society. Thus the scenarios are set out so that they will suggest directions which people can strive to avoid and to achieve. As people act, the probable scenarios for the future will alter.

This does not mean that I have exaggerated the possibilities of failure and success in these scenarios. While the exact direction of change cannot be predicted, the potential for breakdown and hope can be reasonably accurately stated. I fear the possibility for breakdown of the society, for we are continuing to fail to change. I believe in the potential for vast improvement if people would act in the ways which are possible to them.

Futures Conditional, the Northwest Regional Foundation, and I would be interested in receiving scenarios you might write; we shall endeavor to find ways in which the best ones can be published.

1 Entering the Eighties: A Time for Despair

A United Press summary of the experience of the seventies. Embargoed till 1:00 a.m., December 31, 1979.

For the first time in history, we enter a decade without any apparent hope of solving the problems which confront us. The long slide into worldwide disaster has now gone so far that few people have any belief in the potential of the future.

This grim viewpoint appalls the reporter of this summary who is by nature optimistic. However, her conversations with worldwide leaders, intellectuals, and people in the street have produced almost no optimists. Some people, unwilling to give way to despair, hope for a miracle, but no one interviewed could suggest ways in which the extraordinary changes now obviously required could be achieved.

Almost everyone has a different explanation for the 20% unemployment rate, the 35% inflation rate, the continuing 25% annual increase in crime, the breakdown of our local and national governments. (These are U.S. figures, of course, but they reflect worldwide realities.) Different groups concentrate on different symptoms of the overall situation — or metacrisis, as it is now called.

Most citizens still appear to believe that the basic problem is economic. Our difficulties are popularly held to result from the disruptions created by the extraordinary increase in the price of Arab oil and other raw materials during the mid-seventies. The efforts of various countries to counter this pattern did not work and Italy and Portugal both went bankrupt. The impact of national economic collapse in two countries disrupted world trade patterns and created the combined inflation and depression from which we have since suffered.

Those most qualified to analyze our present situation question the reasons for the breakdown: Were they really as simple as this scenario implies or were there far deeper reasons? Some economists are now even willing to admit that our post-war full employment policies may have been a primary cause of the breakdown in our socioeconomic system. They argue that we were caught in a trap in which the only way to keep societies in balance was to ensure continued growth, but that continued growth ceased to be possible in the seventies as we discovered the reality of our finite world.

The majority of economists, however, still insist that there is nothing *really* wrong with their basic model. They see growth and full employment as the norm to which we shall one day return. In general, politicians still agree with the economic profession and they manipulate tax rates, tariff rates, and rates of interest in what has so far been a vain attempt to pull the socioeconomic system out of its continuing deeply depressed state.

Many people seem surprised that the situation continues to worsen despite the change in attitude of the mineral-rich nations. Unfortunately this came so late that it has done little to reverse previous trends. The rich countries and the Arab states are now so hated by the poor countries of the world that cooperation toward more intelligent policies has not been forthcoming and now seems almost impossible.

Indeed, there are a significant number of thinkers who argue that the problems we face are insoluble, not because of economic disasters but because we have not developed leadership styles appropriate to a complex, interdependent world. They argue that the fragmented, bureaucratic approaches developed during the period of economic growth of the industrial era do not permit the consideration of all the interlinked factors which are necessarily involved in the present rapidly changing situation.

From the point of view of this group, the primary

missed opportunity occurred in the mid-seventies. At that time, a large number of people tried to develop new leadership and decision-making styles. The groups active in this process began to comprehend the fundamental problems accompanying the transition from the industrial era to the communications era and to challenge existing leadership groups to explicitly deal with them.

The tunnel-vision of bureaucracies — those in foundations, the media, and government — throttled this effort. The decreasing amount of resources available was concentrated on traditional problems and approaches. New drives and dreams were starved and the movement eventually fell apart.

REACTIONS

During the writing of this wrap-up, I sought reactions from a number of key thinkers who had drawn early attention to the problems from which we are now suffering. Their reactions were uniformly gloomy and depressing.

Robert Heilbroner stated: "In my book, *An Inquiry into the Human Prospect,* published in the mid-seventies, I argued that we could expect to move toward more autocratic and dictatorial governments as a response to predictable crises. I was right about the direction, but wrong about the hoped-for benefits: instead of increased stability and rationality in decision-making, we have moved to a situation where we are apparently totally unable to perceive the central issues."

Dennis Meadows, who worked with others on the Club of Rome project which showed the potential for long-run breakdown in the society, regrets that people did not pay as much attention to the dangers of social collapse as they did to the dangers of economic and ecological imbalance. He argues that our priorities were totally inappropriate during the critical middle years of the seventies when, he believes, it would have been possible to reverse the negative dynamics.

Robert Theobald, author of *An Alternative Future for America's Third Century*, stated that events had unfortunately followed the negative scenarios which he had published during the seventies. "The national and international leadership necessary to realize the potential of the communications era were never developed. As a result the horrendous visions of such writers as Aldous Huxley, George Orwell, and Kurt Vonnegut were essentially realized. The efforts which were made by a number of people to change directions failed to be effective."

DIRECTIONS: INTERNATIONAL

After the collapse of the United Nations in 1978, following the great famine in India when 100 million people died, international communication decreased dramatically. International travel is today highly uncomfortable and often dangerous because of non-exchangeable currencies, out-of-control epidemics, and xenophobia.

Representatives of the rich countries are unwelcome in the poor nations, who feel that the rich countries are primarily responsible for their present intolerable conditions. There have been many lynchings not only in the rural areas but also in some of the major cities.

People from the poor countries have been deeply feared in the rich countries since a large-scale plot to introduce germ-warfare into the United States was discovered. Although it was largely thwarted, paranoia against non-whites continues to develop.

One of the most startling examples of this direction

was the decision of Britain to deport "foreigners" unable to prove that they were born within the United Kingdom. Compared to this step, our draconian crackdown on illegal immigrants appears mild.

WORK/INCOME

The political pressures, which made widespread deportations from the United Kingdom and the United States acceptable, emerged as jobs became scarcer and scarcer during the second half of the seventies. Competition for the right to an income and a meaningful occupation became severe. Elimination of whole categories of job-seekers, such as illegal immigrants, therefore became highly desirable from the point of view of the unions.

It is hard to tell at this point whether people are more threatened by lack of meaningful work or by lack of an income. Kurt Vonnegut is today widely admired for the foresight shown in his science fiction story *Player Piano* in which he stated the danger of loss of purpose in a highly mechanized society without significant activity for the vast majority of the population.

There is as yet little understanding of the factors

which led to the sharp break in economic trends about the mid-seventies. Perhaps the dominant theory is that the Vietnam war disguised the impact of automation and cybernation throughout the sixties and early seventies. The sudden downturn of 1974-75 led companies to adjust their staffing to far more rigorous standards; the resulting higher levels of unemployment have not been overcome in subsequent years.

Simultaneously, many people changed their ideas about desirable standards of living. Instead of spending all their income and fulfilling the prestige criteria of the industrial era, families felt a responsibility to save resources, both to release funds to the poor countries and also to save raw materials for the future. Such decisions, although socially and ecologically responsible, led to a major decrease in demand and a consequent loss of jobs.

CITIES

The nightmare of the cities, repeatedly predicted by study groups during the sixties and seventies, became dramatically obvious in the last five years. Despite all the warning signs, society failed to act. Today, any pretense of law and order has ceased to exist in five cities in America; a similar phenomenon has developed in megalopoli across the world, particularly in the poor countries. The quasi-certainty of this development became clear as early as the seventies when the percentage of accused criminals brought to trial dropped so low that punishment became a lottery.

The destruction of law and order became dramatically obvious in the election year of 1976. The failure to cut into unemployment rates led to a rash of hold-ups.

The name "ghost-city" given to these breakdown areas is actually incorrect. They are not uninhabited, though few would choose to live in them. There is no social order at all; people survive as best they can.

No law enforcement officer with whom this reporter talked saw any chance for a reversal of this situation. Indeed, we seem to be unable, as a society, to mobilize sufficient resources to deal with the seven or eight additional metropolitan areas which are already in danger of a law-and-order breakdown, let alone reversing the consequences of past failures.

HEALTH

Perhaps the most mysterious trend to this reporter, and to many of those she has interviewed, is the extraordinary decrease in life-expectancy in the United States and other rich countries. People throughout the world can now expect to live two years less than they would have as early as 1975.

There are a number of obvious reasons for this change, including the increase in murders, accidents, and suicides. But nobody suggests that these account for all of the change. The most credible reason appears to be the lack of care people exhibit for their own minds and bodies. This is due, perhaps, to their lost respect for themselves and humankind in general after recent discouraging events, especially in the poor countries. Another theory which has been suggested is that doctors are making less effort to keep sick and old people alive.

A companion trend which is far better understood is the drop in the birth-rate. More and more people believe that they have no right to bring children into a world as dangerous as this one. One mother I talked to had always wanted to have three children, and was agonized by her decision to remain childless. Yet, she believed that any other attitude would be totally irresponsible.

Of course, the relatively minor changes in life-expectancy in the rich countries are totally overshadowed by those in the poor countries where epidemics and famine are now continuous. The rise in the death rate has been so dramatic that there has been no increase in the world population over the last five years. Part of this increase in the death rate appears to have been unavoidable because of the negative changes in climate, but deliberate policy changes in the rich countries have contributed to this result.

POLLUTION AND THE ENVIRONMENT

Even at this time when people are deeply pessimistic, this report may seem to some readers to overstate the case. If anything, however, this reporter has underplayed the dangers which have been presented to her.

There is, however, one positive factor. The extraordinary drop in world-wide production has given society more time before it finally exhausts its high-grade resources. Few analysts really believe that humanity will be able to benefit from this development but it is certainly encouraging to be able to find one helpful direction to report.

2 The Impact of the Seventies: Reason for Hope

Computer print out: Designed for high school American Affairs classes. Prepared by Community and Junior College Task Force. January 2, 1980. Access No. 80-7-2-CJC.

Any attempt to set out briefly the direction of the last decade can hardly be expected to be successful. Yet the extent of change in the seventies has been so extraordinary that it is certainly necessary to try to provide some handles for ensuring better understandings.

The Bicentennial Era movement is now seen as the primary factor which altered the dynamics of American society. People today believe that just as it took fifteen years to create the country and to obtain acceptance of the Constitution and the Bill of Rights, it will take as long to comprehend the extraordinary alterations in our ways of thinking and action required by our movement into the communications era. Millions of people are today involved in the "Creating America's Third Century" movement which is designed to promote citizen participation activities.

Each of you reading this document will have been affected by some of the changes which have occurred as our basic understandings of society altered. Some of you will have benefited from the changing relationships between work and income distribution which developed in the last half of the seventies. Almost all of you will have found your patterns of education shifting as society became more convinced of the need to integrate learning with other activities.

For many people, the degree and direction of change is almost incredibly large — and all too often deeply shocking. On the other hand, there are many people who find the new interdependent society welcome and desirable. For this reason, discussions of these issues require particular care in order to preserve the win-win relationships of dialogue and to avoid the win-lose confrontation styles characteristic of the industrial era. Only in this way can everyone learn the scope and direction of the shift in values and direction which has taken place and is in process.

Few people in the mid-seventies expected the hopeful directions which have emerged in the last five years. There was little understanding of the possibility of rapid restructuring of systems: The classical paper by John Platt, entitled *Hierarchical Reconstruction*, did not become well known until 1976.

One way of describing the revolutionary change in consciousness appears to be the re-understanding of the importance of religious values (as separate from dogma). Politicians as well as churchmen learned that honesty, responsibility, humility, love, and a respect for mystery were all required if societies were to be functional. As this perception developed, the manipulative patterns which were dominant during the late-industrial era came to be seen as increasingly counter-productive.

As a result of this religious revival, we began to perceive that each of us could achieve more for ourselves and for others if we would work together and stop fighting with each other. We began to perceive that cooperative styles were more effective than competitive ones. We also began to see just how deeply our culture was permeated with the competitive spirit and considered cooperation effete and sissy. For example, schools run by middle-class whites for American Indians often stressed competitive sports: Those in charge of the schools were appalled by the fact that competition was considered inappropriate by Indian groups. One of the indicators of success for those in charge of these institutions was the speed at which the competitive spirit could be imbued; there was no understanding of the consequent destruction of the Indian's perceptual world.

We have rejected the idea that the only way to motivate people to change was to force them to act out of fear or to reward them for their actions with a specific payment, either physical or psychological. We have discovered that people will rise to challenge if they are given the opportunity to do so. One of the more surprising developments of the past five years is that we have found that thinkers who were assumed to have totally different concepts were actually moving in converging directions. This was particularly true of Maslow and Skinner, who were previously seen as making different statements about human motivation and are now perceived as using similar approaches but starting their work from different historical vantage points.

This change in understanding is still not, of course, complete. Many still argue that a belief in the ability of man to rise to challenge is naive because it is unreal to expect that everybody will take advantage of new opportunities. Two responses are relevant. First, it is indeed true that many people have been educated in ways which deprived them of leadership skills; opportunities therefore need to be developed for those who have the ability to learn to learn. Second, we must accept the reality that some people will always waste their potentials of freedom. It is increasingly agreed, however, that the cost of this waste will always be less than that which occurs when people are prevented from using their creativity and imagination by a closed bureaucratic system.

The religious/psychological rhetoric used so far makes many people acutely uncomfortable. Some analysts therefore prefer to start their thinking from the need to manage the world more effectively than has been the case in the past. They argue that bureaucratic decision-making has been proved to be ineffective and that new forms of management are required which will permit us to ensure the needed changes.

Such management systems require effective decision-making and the bringing together of people who trust each other; otherwise, fear will distort information flows. Trust can only be generated when people are willing to act responsibly with each other rather than fearing each other.

SPECIFIC DEVELOPMENTS

Introduction of guaranteed income and committed spending

We have discovered in the last five years, of course,

that a system based on job-holding, on the fear of being fired and the hope of promotion is not an effective way of getting things done. By the mid-seventies, most people were so busy trying to hold onto their jobs that they had no time to do their potentially meaningful work. Indeed, the extraordinary irrelevance of many jobs to the real needs of the society was one of the primary realities which forced reconsideration of our economic system.

Limited forms of a guaranteed income (basic economic security) were introduced in the mid-seventies because of the continuing unemployment problem. The rationale for this action was the experiments conducted during the late sixties and early seventies in several U.S. cities. These showed that people did not automatically "goof off" if they received their income as a right. The original guaranteed income plans were rapidly extended during the last five years as we discovered that people were willing to do necessary work even though their income was not tied to a specific job.

At the same time, new measures were introduced which permitted people to move in and out of the job market far more freely. It has been recognized that people need opportunities to broaden their education and their experience at several points during their career. Thus, people today accumulate educational credits during their work which can be cashed in to provide for low-cost continuing education or a sabbatical.

It is now possible to state that acute financial poverty has been eliminated in the United States. Instead of the dire results so often predicted, it seems clear that more of the work needed by the society has been accomplished in recent years. People have indeed risen to challenge, once given an income base on which they could rely.

But while it has been possible to abolish poverty in the United States, conditions in the rest of the world remain highly unsatisfactory. Nevertheless, the recognition of limits to growth, the developing understanding of the concept of enoughness, and the placing of a floor under the incomes of all citizens has significantly improved the relationships between rich and poor countries. A constructive debate is emerging around the concept of "enoughness" which is generally assumed to mean that each of us should be able to obtain what we need but not what we want. Even economists, who tend to reject this approach because it destroys much of the underpinnings of their discipline, are beginning to see its necessity.

Life-long learning

By the mid-seventies, schools and colleges across the country were in desperate straits. Those within educational institutions found that they were "reality-poor," i.e., their teaching did not deal with the patterns which were developing during the transition from the industrial era to the communications era. In addition, schools in many of the large cities became highly dangerous due to very high crime rates.

The origin of the reversal of this situation is rather widely laid to the creation of the *Classes of '76* model in conjunction with the Bicentennial. The idea of this program was that all educational institutions should reconsider the appropriate form of education for a rapidly changing world because it was no longer possible to argue that the old automatically knew and that the young should learn, but that both needed to learn in concert.

Every educational institution from kindergarten through adult education was challenged to use commencement day in 1976 and subsequent years to communicate about their learnings. A study of papers and magazines of this year shows that different educational groups used every conceivable means of communication from buttons to speeches, from Tshirts to ballet, from painting and drama to the writing of articles and books.

The result of this process was to challenge effectively the concept that education should take place during certain clearly-defined periods of school and college — that life, work, and learning could be separated. During the past five years, we have moved steadily toward life-long learning based on an understanding that each person needs to be able to continue to learn about developments in our constantly changing world.

Education is more often integrated into life. Courses taught on campus are made available to the community through audio-tape, video-tape, and two-way cable capacity. Fewer and fewer people teach full-time; more and more work in their own fields within the community and also teach students. Most classrooms now contain people of many life stages for it has been found that the consequent increase in diversity opens up far better possibilities for dialogue.

Perhaps, most importantly, education has once again become passionate. It is understood that learning requires the involvement both of brain and heart. Disagreements are expected. It is the working through of these disagreements, together with opportunities for action to clarify the insights gained through difference of opinion, which is now seen by most people to be at the heart of the understanding and decision-making system.

One of the primary learnings of the past five years has been a clear perception of the difference between education and training. Education is the process of understanding a subject from the inside so that we can participate in its further development. Training is the process of learning from the outside in order to attain a necessary skill. It follows that any particular subject can be perceived as either education or training, depending on an individual's goals. Thus a bridge designer will see engineering as education and languages, in order to learn about bridges, as training. A linguist will see foreign languages as education and learning enough mechanics to make his appliances run as training. Whatever the subject chosen, however, almost everyone now agrees that society has an obligation to educate each person in at least one subject.

Relationships between rich and poor countries

At the beginning of the seventies, most leaders and thinkers throughout the world still agreed that economic growth was a primary necessity for both rich and poor countries. It was argued that the poor countries could and should catch up to the standards of the rich. This approach continued despite the fact that the gap between the rich and the poor countries grew increasingly wide during the post World-War II world.

The dominant view is now profoundly different. The rich countries have realized their need for fundamental change in such fields as work, income distribution, and education. They are therefore prepared to admit that the poor countries need to follow a different developmental route than that which occurred in the nineteenth century in the rich countries.

The result of this shift in perception has been profoundly positive. Both rich and poor countries have been prepared to examine again their views about indicators of growth and welfare. It is no longer believed that the Gross National Product measures satisfaction. It follows, therefore, that it no longer makes sense to argue that the standard of living, let alone the quality of life, in the rich countries is five, ten, or fifty times higher than that of the poor countries. Indeed, quality of life indicators now being developed show that the gap between the rich and the poor countries may not even exist. There are an increasing number of observers who claim that the rich countries may have further to go to reach a human society than the poor.

Nevertheless, the rich and the poor country debate remains heated despite these new insights. Even at this time when both the industrialized and the raw-material-rich countries have committed themselves to helping the poor countries, it will take ten to fifteen years to eliminate extreme poverty in the world. We are learning that the costs of rapid growth are too high to be tolerable — that the consequent destruction of a culture creates far more damage than can be balanced by more rapid economic growth. Our best hope for significant change results from the drop in the birth rate which is now dramatic and is still accelerating.

Religion as a driving force

In the early seventies, the main-line Protestant denominations as well as the Catholics seemed to be losing strength rapidly and dramatically. On the other hand, the fundamentalist sects seemed to be gaining ground.

The Bicentennial provided an extraordinary impetus

to change in this area. It was remembered that one of the primary factors behind the American revolution was the churches which justified an end to allegiance to George III and helped create a loyalty to America. As their historical revolutionary role was increasingly understood, clergymen then began to examine how the churches could play a role in facilitating the twentieth-century transition from the industrial era to the communications era.

As could have been expected, a revolutionary role calling for an emphasis on values was unacceptable to many church members who felt that a demand for religion seven days a week was either unnecessary or unfair. On the other hand, many people who had left the established church returned and were willing to commit both more time and more energy to the churches, which have now become once again a major force on the North American continent.

Government

The greatest shift of all has developed in our patterns of government. In the mid-seventies, there were calls for centralized, dictatorial control in the belief that democracy had broken down. Today, we are aware that only democracy, in its profound sense, can ensure accurate movement of information and effective decision-making. We have come to understand the meaning behind Churchill's statement that "Democracy is the worst form of government except all the others."

The failures of centralized government are now better understood. Lord Acton's statement, "Power tends to corrupt and absolute power corrupts absolutely," has been updated to read "Power tends to distort information and absolute power distorts information absolutely."

Each of us is aware of the process of distortion today. Understanding this problem has become a critical part of the curriculum in the last five years. We know that if we are afraid of those who hold authority, we begin to tell them what we believe they want to know. If we are completely afraid of them, we think of nothing else except how to please them. Both those who hold authority and those who do not are helping to build institutional systems which encourage the effective movement of information and prevent distortion.

When people began to understand this problem, there were many who feared that the result would be the destruction of all authority systems and a consequent inability to make decisions. We have found, however, that people are willing to accept learning and guidance from those who do really know. Our willingness to accept and use knowledge has revolutionized both local and national government. (For a full statement of progress in this area, see 79-5-754/NEA.)

PART II: Problems and Possibilities

The pieces which follow have been developed by me in recent years for a variety of audiences. They range from 500 words to 5,000, from highly formal presentations to very informal ones. Taken together, they give some sense of my hopes and my fears, my perceptions of the possibilities for action and my frustrations when we fail to move at times when intelligent change is possible.

Much of the material in this part of the book was originally developed in the context of the trend letter, *Futures Conditional,* edited by Jeanne Scott and myself during the years 1973-1974. These pieces are not designed to form a coherent whole. Rather, I hope that you will find a number of thoughts which catch your imagination, which force you to look again at a situation which you thought you understood fully. In many ways this book is designed to make you feel that others besides yourself may be right in any particular situation.

I have adopted this approach because I am convinced that most of us need to re-examine with care the beliefs by which we live. Only when we have done this can we learn to pull together a coherent worldview which will make sense of the apparent breakdown of our world.

3 Communication Realities and the Conservative Revolution

How would you like to be able to determine this or that? To me it seems that a more pertinent question would be 'How would you like someone else to answer . . . questions for you?' And it would almost certainly be somebody else.

Joseph Wood Krutch

Written especially for this volume in February 1975, this piece is designed to lead us to rethink what alliances toward change are possible. I have deliberately used the word "conservative" in this piece despite the drive of many to equate the conservative and the reactionary: I believe that the word "conservative" is too valuable to be thrown away. The piece should be seen as an introduction to this part of this volume.

Today we are all bombarded with communications. Each of us needs to be alert to extraordinary amounts of information just to stay alive in this society, let alone to avoid problems or to take advantage of possibilities. We can see this reality all around us: One dramatic piece of evidence is the failure of many citizens to take advantage of government programs specifically designed to aid them because, despite all efforts, they remain unaware of their entitlements.

The overload of information is numbing us to the critical messages about continuing change which we ought to be receiving. Most people are not aware of the new directions which are developing and therefore act in ways which are not congruent with their own self-interest. It is, however, difficult to break through the overload problem because those who can afford the cost of access to the media trumpet their conventional messages so loudly that those who have new ideas but little money go unheard.

Even more seriously, the levels of distrust in the society are now so great that many messages are today ignored or denied because of the relationship between the sender and the receiver. It is assumed that most people are trying to manipulate others to suit their purposes rather than moving accurate information about new possibilities and problems. One is reminded of the old story about two psychiatrists who ride in an elevator and, as they reach their floor, the operator says "Good Morning." As they walk down the hall, one says to the other, "Now what did she mean by that?"

Effective communication requires that the receiver of a message believes the sender to be trying to send accurate information. It is not, of course, necessary that the information actually be completely accurate

— indeed, this is impossible. The problem is that for several decades society has accepted and encouraged deliberate distortion of the truth to ensure that the goals of those with power be reached. The primary consequence of this pattern of distortion has been the growing distrust in our society of all information, and a profound shift in political perceptions has therefore occurred.

For the first time in several decades, most Americans do not believe that additional government programs are the answer to all our ills. People are looking for ways to return power and responsibility to the individual, the family, the group, and the community. This new direction constitutes a "conservative" revolution. Using the word "conservative" in a positive sense runs counter to present directions; however, I believe it is a good word to save.

Our present culture depends on government intervention when things go wrong rather than on citizen education and action designed to make things go right. To deal with the crises which are now developing, we must provide accurate information to citizens and create real opportunities for people to be involved in changing directions on the basis of this information.

The present energy crisis provides a test case for our directions. The dominant approach is coercive — whether it be through higher prices or through gas rationing. The conservative believes instead that people first need to be clearly informed of the reality of the energy crisis and its possible repercussions and then be challenged to make responsible decisions to reduce their energy use.

The conservative view is considered infeasible in Washington, where they argue that "voluntarism has failed." They do not recognize that the confusion of information which is now rampant makes it impossible for people to make effective decisions: The government insists there is a shortage of fuel while oil and gas companies encourage use. I recently saw a sign: "Lots of gas — shortage of customers." In addition, while people are asked to save energy, they are encouraged to buy more goods and services. They rightly understand that more goods and services use more energy. We cannot claim to have tried voluntarism until we provide accurate, understandable information to people and challenge them to act responsibly on it.

The conservative position becomes more credible when we remember the winter of 1973-74. Although

Congress and the President were unable to agree on the required policies, citizens voluntarily cut back on oil and gas use. We can assume that this discipline would have continued if the need for conservation were still set out clearly.

Today, in many fields, we face a clear choice — we can begin to rely on genuine education of citizens or we can continue with ever more drastic manipulations of the socioeconomy by a small minority. While increasing numbers of people call for less government intervention, we continue to develop programs which lessen freedom. Most of our decision-making is based on the assumption that the individual, the family, the group, and the community must somehow be saved from the consequences of their own folly.

Conservatives do not, of course, suggest that all individual decisions would be wise. But they do argue that the overall impact of an educational approach would be more satisfactory than the results which can be expected on the basis of our present interventionist policies. They argue that policies which are designed to save people from the consequences of their own folly are usually not effective; indeed that they all too often increase the social problems they are designed to cure.

The policies which we have developed to deal with identified social problems have created new situations which are often worse than the original problem. For example, present welfare programs designed to deal with poverty have made self-reliance almost impossible for the poor. Our income distribution system is based on the belief that those who receive money from it are idle, irresponsible bums; thus the systems we have created force people to become idle and irresponsible. In effect, government programs create self-fulfilling prophecies — they force people to accept the assumptions made about them.

Conservatives accept the fact that our interventionist directions have not been effective. But this does not imply that they accept the opposite argument — that if we sweep away all the policies which have been introduced in the post-war years, the socioeconomy would function well. They do not believe that all our present problems result from excessive intervention and would vanish if we recreated a free market system.

The true conservative knows that we cannot go back. S/he knows that we have moved too far to be able to survive using the competitive styles of the industrial era. S/he knows that the decisions of humanity have created a new, crowded — indeed overcrowded — world; knows that we can only deal with the issues which now face us if we consciously struggle toward a new interdependent, cooperative style. From the very beginnings of the human race, humanity has divided itself into in-groups and out-groups. The rules for interaction *within* an in-group have often been sharply different from those defined as appropriate for interaction *between* an in-group and an out-group. Indeed, the in-group has often been defined as human while the out-group has been denied that standing. Torture and murder have been accepted as appropriate for out-groups even when they are utterly rejected within the in-group.

This split between "we" and "they" is no longer viable. We cannot accord lesser rights to one set of human beings compared to another. We cannot have one set of rules for "friends" and another for "enemies." We must learn what Pogo meant when he stated that "We have met the enemy and they is us."

We are learning the necessity of diversity. We are learning that a monolithic culture is as vulnerable to crisis as a single crop system is to pests and blight. We are discovering the importance of the availability of different views about appropriate directions. Only as we understand this reality will we be able to bring people together to choose common directions despite their differences.

In summary then, we need to reject both of the political views which are presently dominant: that there is an effective policy which will solve every problem, and that problems will solve themselves without the need for leadership. We must struggle to understand creatively the new institutions we shall need if we are to manage the extraordinarily rapid change which is now taking us from the industrial era to the communications era. This task can only be achieved if we provide citizens with meaningful information and opportunities for involvement.

4 Environmental Agreements

. . . exponential curves grow to infinity only in mathematics. In the physical world they either turn around and saturate, or they break down catastrophically. It is our duty as thinking men to do our best toward a gentle saturation, instead of sustaining the exponential growth, though this faces us with very unfamiliar and distasteful problems.

Dennis Gabor

This editorial from the April 1974 issue of *Futures Conditional* suggests that we are making progress in understanding our situation even though policy-makers continue to ignore the new learnings. Economists and ecologists could see that their understandings were convergent if they would listen to each other instead of arguing with each other.

Slowly, and with great difficulty, certain minimal agreements are emerging in the field of energy and the environment. Heated arguments still rage around each of these statements, but the movement toward convergence appears to be irreversible.

The first agreement is that continuation of the present rate of waste for any lengthy period — even one generation — would make the achievement of a reasonable standard of living and the preservation of a viable environment impossible.

Second, there are enormous technical and social difficulties in achieving a rate of growth in production of food, fiber, and manufactured goods adequate to keep up with the present rate of increase in population.

Third, long-continued high rates of economic growth are infeasible because of ecological constraints; thus it becomes vital that we decrease rates of population growth so as to prevent famine and preserve the environment.

It may seem that these agreements are too limited to be useful in discussion and policy-making. But this is, in fact, not the case. Once we fully accept the validity of these minimal statements, we can no longer shelter behind the conventional wisdom which still places maximum rates of economic growth at the heart of government policy-making.

Well over 90% of our present discussions and writings are irrelevant, for they try to preserve a socio-economic system which has vanished beyond recall. For example, we must recognize that we cannot rebuild our present international exchange mechanisms, for they reflect a society in which economic affairs always have prime importance. Similarly, we cannot "afford" to cut unemployment to tolerable levels, for our social structures have made increasingly high levels of unemployment necessary to avoid inflation.

In effect, the minimal agreements we are reaching make it possible for us to discover the fundamental question that now exists: What forms of society and economy will/must replace those which our very success has made obsolete? Any discussion or action which does not *fully* accept this reality is doomed to futility and failure.

While we can now state the fundamental question, we have few policy responses because we have so far failed to put in the necessary effort. We need to break up the general question in ways which will point toward the areas in which we must act responsibly and immediately if we are to assure the future of planet Earth.

I am convinced that much of our societal frustration today stems from one fundamental cause. We believe that the answers to our problems are known and that failures to apply these answers represent the results of incompetence, irresponsibility, or ill will. If all of us could recognize the real newness of our situation, we might become more tolerant of our failures to discover instantaneous solutions.

5 The Temporary Becomes Permanent

Among the important respects in which industrial society differs significantly from all the societies that went before, perhaps the most significant, is that it has institutionalized secular, manipulative rationality, and thus both economic and technological development. The basic trends of Western society, most of which can be traced back as far as the twelfth or eleventh centuries, can be seen as part of a common, complex trend of interacting events. . . . These processes of change, each facilitating the other, have become routinely—one might even say inexorably—cumulative. It is well known that, as a result, the rate of change of many aspects of social life has become exponential.

Herman Kahn and Anthony J. Wiener

This editorial from the November 1973 issue of *Futures Conditional* provides the counterpoint to the previous piece. It shows the unthinking stupidity of bureaucracies and their unwillingness/inability to think about the real situations now emerging. Incidentally, the editorial notes the threat of a major recession at a time when we were still being assured that no significant downturn was possible because of our understanding of economic forces.

The title of this piece which echoes a French saying, *C'est seulement le temporaire qui dure*, reflects more than cynicism. In effect, it represents the "realities" of policy-making as we now experience them. We shall briefly examine the ways in which temporary fixes in economic policy, particularly in the area of consumption, threaten to become permanent.

When something starts to go wrong, policy-makers are far more likely to resort to a quick fix of the apparent situation, a quick "answer" to a problem, than to examine what is actually happening. The fix, once adopted, becomes the focus of attention an increasing amount of effort is devoted to ensuring the continued viability of the temporary measure. All too often the temporary fix thus comes to determine the shape of future decisions.

Meanwhile, the basic forces which required the initial adoption of the fix usually grow in intensity and seriousness. These forces are, however, often ignored because the attention of the society is increasingly concentrated on the fix which has, in theory, dealt with the problem.

Our present patterns of consumption, production, and other economic activities result from a long series of technological fixes. Unless we refocus our attention on the real situation today, we shall almost certainly create a socioeconomic crisis of the magnitude of the thirties. Such a crisis may or may not take the form of a major depression, although this is indeed possible. Certainly it would cause social disruption comparable to that which developed some forty-five years ago.

How can we learn to understand the forces which are presently controlling us and the threats they pose? In order to identify and analyze them we need to place our present situation in historical perspective. In the Middle Ages, people were considered to be permanently fixed in the specific niche in society to which they were born. All classes in the society, rich or poor, were considered to have reciprocal rights and responsibilities.

From our vantage point today this concept of society is inequitable and constraining. Our present underlying societal theory is that in our equalitarian system everybody competes on an equal basis; poverty is therefore the fault of the individual, and the suffering which results from this poverty is inevitable. In the Middle Ages, on the other hand, poverty was considered a failure of the *society*, and the rich therefore had an obligation to relieve the misery of the poor.

During the transition from the Middle Ages through

the mercantile period to the industrial era, the traditional medieval patterns of rights and responsibilities were gradually dissipated. Those with drive and initiative in all classes found the existing societal framework unbearably constraining and worked to achieve greater freedom to do what they personally wished. The have-nots were seen as failures to be manipulated and oppressed.

A new type of society thus came into existence. The neo-classical economic theory developed in the late nineteenth century provided an elegant conceptual justification for a world with great extremes of wealth and poverty, of power and weakness. Neo-classical theory "proved" that, given certain conditions, the amount of money earned by an individual reflected exactly his contribution to the creation of resources in the society.

Such a theory served the needs of the time very efficiently. The economic theoreticians argued that nothing could be done to change conditions without weakening the economic drive of the system, which was believed to be of primary importance. Later economists, although aware that this theory was not applicable to real conditions, seldom pointed this out. They therefore made it possible to ignore the fact that the distribution of income depended, as it had always done in reality, on the distribution of power in the society. Those with power gain large amounts of resources and those without power have little.

Despite the rhetoric of economists and politicians, many people were aware of the radical injustice of the early twentieth century economic style. There was widespread unrest which was only diffused by the long-run consequences of Henry Ford's five-dollar day. Ford saw correctly that mass production was totally dependent on mass distribution and that mass distribution would only be possible if larger wages were paid to workers. The five-dollar day was the first step into a new socioeconomic system where an ever-increasing number of people could afford a growing amount of goods and services and thus purchase an ever-larger amount of available products.

The system worked without conscious government intervention until the beginning of the 1930s, when it broke down dramatically. John Maynard Keynes, the British economist, theorized that no automatic mechanism existed to balance production and consumption. He stated that recessions were therefore inevitable *unless* society acted to keep consumption growing as rapidly as possible. This led to the theory and creation of a consumption society. The viability of our socioeconomic system became increasingly dependent on increases in consumption.

For many years we enjoyed being manipulated into consumption. Wasn't a television set good for those long evenings when we had nothing to do? Wasn't it better to have two television sets so that people in the family could watch different programs if they wanted to do so — and wouldn't the ideal be everyone with their own television set?

But by the 1960s we had begun to ask ourselves what we had given up when we acquired multiple television sets. We began to think that it might be better to buy goods and services *only* if they served our own style of living.

A consumers' revolt started tentatively, and it is still gathering momentum; people are buying the goods which satisfy them rather than those which are prestigious in the eyes of their neighbors and the society in general.

The consumers' revolt now threatens the stability of the present socioeconomic system. Instead of being manipulable through advertising and other propaganda, people are making their own judgments. Even the importance of meat and the automobile, which once seemed central to the American dream, is being challenged. Patterns of consumption are changing, partly because of the rise in prices but also because of changing perceptions of what is important.

The result is rapid variations in consumer behavior, thus undermining our present socioeconomy which can only distribute goods and services efficiently if there are enough jobs, which in turn requires that we all remain willing to maintain these jobs by buying more and more goods and services — that we do not cut back because of changing tastes or our concern for ecology or our worries about the uncertainty of the present situation.

Even more seriously, our economic system is based on a win-lose model of reality. Everyone tries to get more at the expense of somebody else. Our economic system does not permit operation of a win-win model, where we would all gain through the successful operation of the system.

We can only escape from this highly undesirable situation if we fundamentally rethink our patterns of socioeconomic activity. We must realize that there are no narrow economic answers to our present situation, that we can only begin to resolve our problems on the basis of new ways of seeing success and new patterns of organization of our socioeconomic system. Only two of the most basic changes can be mentioned here.

— We need to create an ethic which is based on a belief in "enoughness": We need to understand that having more than this amount of resources is as life-impeding as having too little. Ironically, many of the poor countries of the world previously have lived within an enoughness ethic.

—We need to create a work ethic through which people do things they find important and therefore do well. The loss of pride in work is making it impossible to carry out even those activities which are truly essential for man's survival.

Both of these proposals are compromises between two extreme views. In the area of work, one group argues that people should work because it is good for them, and the more unpleasant the work the better it will be for them. The other argues that people should "do their own thing." The proposal made here suggests that there is always work which needs to be done, but that skills and concerns of people can be meshed with the work in such a way that people will enjoy what they do.

In the area of consumption, one group argues that we should cut consumption to a minimum, and another that consumption is good in itself. The view advanced here views consumption as a means by which people can more effectively develop themselves and their society, i.e., consumption is a means and not an end.

All the technological fixes we have introduced in economics increase the necessity for, and the intensity of, competition. They make the balance and cooperation we so urgently need more and more difficult. The creation of a functional, effective socioeconomic system requires change in our ethical values as well as in our techniques. Real improvement in our economic situation must be preceded by a reexamination of our values.

6 Citizen Participation or Fascism?

Men can tolerate extraordinary hardship if they think that it is an unalterable part of life's travail, but an administered frustration—unsanctioned by religion or custom or deeply rooted values—is more than the spirit can bear. So increasingly men rage at all kinds of institutions, here and around the world. Most of them have no clear vision of the kind of world they want to build; they only know that they don't want the kind of world they have.

John W. Gardner

The tension between the behavior of bureaucracies, educators, politicians, and the media, on the one hand, and our changing understandings of the nature of humanity on the other were explored in this July 1974 editorial. The risk of fascism was contrasted with the potential of a more humane and participatory society.

I have been concerned with two main themes in the past three years. First, what should be the changes in policies and values as we move from the industrial era to the communications era? Second, how can we hope to bring about these changes in policies and values?

Until very recently, these concerns seemed peripheral because everybody was so busy arguing whether it was, in reality, necessary to change policies and industrial-era values fundamentally. Relatively suddenly, we seem to have reached a new comprehension of our situation. We are coming to understand that we do face a major crisis and that action to deal with this crisis is urgent.

It may perhaps be useful to cite two examples of this developing insight. Recently, James Reston wrote a column in which he contrasted the impeachment procedure of President Nixon in the United States with the "impeachment" of the rich countries now being conducted in the United Nations by the poor countries. He argued that the unwillingness of the media to pay attention to the charges against what are sometimes called the "over-developed nations" could lead to very serious problems in the immediate future.

The second example of this theme of major, immediate change was developed at the first international symposium of the Environmental Series just completed in Spokane. Representatives of various fundamentally divergent views about the future came together to look at the "Dilemma of Mankind." Almost all those present agreed that only major immediate change in policies could prevent serious breakdowns and possible total catastrophe.

There was one clear exception to this view, and it was put forward by those who had been asked to come to the symposium to advance the economic growth viewpoint. These speakers argued that it was possible for world population to increase to a level of 20 or 30 billion and that it would be possible to provide a standard of living comparable to the present American level for such a world population size.

The divergence between these views, one which called for immediate change and the other which stated the possibility of continued economic growth for some time into the future, at first sight seemed so great that the meshing of policy appeared impossible. However, the effect of compound interest is so great that these positions actually lead to related conclusions about appropriate action at the present time. At the current rate of growth, the population of the world would exceed 31.2 billion in less than a hundred years. It therefore follows, even from the economic growth viewpoint, that it would be necessary to begin to change policy during the lifetimes of those now being educated.

Both schools of thought can therefore agree that

we should start providing new understandings and knowledge which will permit people to begin to comprehend the issues involved in limiting growth rather than perpetuating those views which existed during the post-World War II period of continuous economic growth. As the movement of this changed pattern of information continues, we shall find the resolution of the differences between those who would stop growth *now* and those who believe that it can continue for a period into the future.

We are therefore past the time when it is useful to argue whether major change is required; the issues are the time span over which changes must be made as well as the type of changes needed. Hidden behind this issue, however, is the critical question which is a new primary dividing point: Is it reasonable to expect existing institutional structures to play a leading role in bringing about the necessary changes? Or must we develop new methods of moving information and creating coalitions as compared to those which have become dominant in the industrial era?

It was this question which led to the most heated arguments during the first international symposium in Spokane. One group argued that bureaucratic structures, public and private, are the only ones with power at the present time and that there is therefore no real choice but to rely on them to move information — and, if this is not sufficient, to force required changes. Those who disagreed with this approach believed that this route necessarily led to fascism. They also argued that it was infeasible, as bureaucracies are designed to prevent change and to preserve the status quo.

I believe it is crucial that we recognize the centrality of this question and the different directions which can be expected to result from the choices we make. It is all too possible that we may decide by default that people are too stupid to understand the issues of today. We shall then drift into situations where institutional structures are permitted to force change which they assume is valuable. Orwell assumed in his book *1984* that we would move in this direction and there is certainly no clear-cut evidence that we have rejected it.

I believe that fascism is both undesirable and ineffective, that it can be proved that our only hope of changing with sufficient rapidity is to develop increased public participation based on each person's competence and knowledge. This is the way to transform present problems into possibilities.

Unfortunately, the significance of our question and

the clearcut choices we need to make are disguised by the present abuse of the rhetoric of "public participation." More and more communities are spending more and more time "involving" their citizens. Typically the citizenry are asked to work through a highly complex questionnaire or other process which provides "objective" information to the existing leadership about citizen views of the critical choices which exist for their community.

Those who use this kind of "involvement" fully intend to enhance the democratic process. Unfortunately, the primary result of such efforts has often been to weaken the necessary *ongoing* discussion by which new facts, ideas, and dreams can be continuously incorporated into a community's planning as they develop.

We need to become very clearly aware of our success criteria as we talk about citizen participation and involvement. Are we simply trying to ensure the flow of more complete information to a small, closed elite who will use it to make decisions? Or are we trying to increase the number of persons who are informed and engaged in the decision-making process so that all those who are competent and willing to be involved can be fully engaged in thinking and acting to create the future?

We must find a way to create ad-hoc organizations which will unite those people and groups willing to break through the barriers to change in which we are all caught. As we build these new coalitions, we shall be continuously surprised by those who choose to ally themselves with the change process and continuously disappointed by those who, when confronted with real effective options, opt out. Indeed, it may well be that our present perceptions of who are the "good guys" and the "bad guys" form one of the major blocks against creating effective action coalitions. It is not necessarily those who talk loudest or most liberally about the present situation who are most willing to act.

We must recognize that the central question of our time is the nature of "authority." We are therefore being forced to challenge present authority structures. It would be unreasonable to expect existing authority structures to respond to this challenge with great enthusiasm. Nevertheless, many of those now serving in these authority structures may be willing to join in the challenge if we can develop appropriate ad-hoc organizations in which they can operate effectively.

7 The Impact of Violence

I do not wish to seem overdramatic, but I can only conclude from the information available to me as Secretary-General that the Members of the United Nations have perhaps ten years left in which to subordinate their ancient quarrels and launch a global partnership to curb the arms race, to improve the human environment, to defuse the population explosion, and to supply the required momentum to development efforts. If such a global partnership is not forged within the next decade, then I very much fear that the problems I have mentioned will have reached such staggering proportions that they will be beyond our capacity to control.

U Thant
May 1969

The risk of fascism and the potential for a more human society forces us to clarify our ideas about the impact of violence on decision-making. The best definition of violence that I know was developed at a seminar at Northwestern University: "Violence is harm done to the notion of person, whether physically or mentally." This definition helps us to perceive that the notion of violence is profoundly subjective and personal. It follows that violence is more and more infeasible as we move into an increasingly interdependent and dangerous world, for what some see as a reasonable use of power may be perceived by others as totally unacceptable patterns of violence. This April 1973 article, written at the end of direct American participation in the Vietnam war, explores the issues of violence and non-violence.

As we turn our attention away from the running psychological sores of the last decade, we discover numerous crises which have already developed so far that they threaten the stability of our internal and international socioeconomic systems.

We have no articulated philosophy which promises to provide solutions for today's real world. The 19th-century ideal of dependence on individual self-reliance is obviously ineffective in today's highly interdependent communications era. Only an understanding of the need and potential of cooperation will be effective in today's conditions.

Cooperation and violence cannot intermix, however. This reality creates one of our meta-crises. The internal and international socioeconomic systems of the West have been primarily based on the right to violence. If negotiation and compromise failed, it was accepted that the power of the groups involved would be tested through force, e.g., strikes internally and war externally.

This style of behavior is, in many ways, merely an extension of the patterns which are used by animals to establish dominance. The extent of the territory of solitary animals contracts and expands on the basis of their relative strength compared to their neighbors.

Animals which live in groups usually have a pattern which ensures that younger, stronger males challenge the older, wiser leader. When the cunning of the old no longer matches the energy of the young, there is a change in leadership.

Violence has always been one of the causes contributing to ecological and human balancing processes. Today it threatens to destroy with finality any balance. Mankind, through its development of sophisticated techniques, has removed itself from the natural restraints which have previously limited the destructive potential of all species.

One of the ways that man has disrupted previous relationships is obvious and much discussed: We now have the destructive capacity to kill all life on earth several times over by using nuclear weapons. There is also the potential for death inherent in biological and chemical weaponry. Mankind has recognized his "incredible" power to destroy; we have now reached the point where the major factor preventing the use of force is the mutual fear of the destructive power available. We did not dare to "bomb Vietnam back into the stone age" for such a decision could conceivably have set off a nuclear holocaust.

The increase in our potential for violence is, however, less important than the increase in our communications ability. It was said 200 years ago that the shot fired in Concord, Massachusetts was "heard around the world." The statement is true but the delays were very long. Today, any major event anywhere in the world impacts *immediately* on the rest of the world, and each significant event is inextricably caught up in the total pattern.

A startling example of this reality surfaced when President Sadat of Egypt announced some time ago that he had delayed hostilities in the Middle East because the world was preoccupied with events elsewhere. He judged that the importance of the "communication" involved in the renewal of hostilities would not have been perceived.

The necessary conclusion is that international violence in today's conditions is a *means* of drawing attention to a situation and of stating the seriousness with which the group or the individual regards his cause. Violence is not essentially a way of settling disputes; it is a statement about the breakdown of relationships.

Unfortunately, while violence may start as a planned communication, it has its own dynamics. If a disagreement is not settled, its scope grows with time as communication is frustrated. Compromises, which might have been acceptable originally, become intolerable.

The SALT talks aiming at arms limitation are a recognition of the infeasibility of violence between powers with nuclear arms. The drive toward detente between China, Russia, and America follows from a recognition that conflict between any two powers may embroil the third and lead to the nuclear war everybody fears.

There is no certainty that the commitment to peace which now exists between the great powers will be sufficient to overcome the real causes of international tension. The interests of the rich and the poor countries of the world do diverge sharply. The tensions between these two groups can be expected to become more serious as we recognize the changing balance of power resulting from the developing shortages of raw materials in many of the rich areas.

Even if detente should be achieved, this alone will not be sufficient to ensure the end of violence. There are new realities today. We now know that determined guerrillas and terrorists can only be stopped in ways which disrupt the complex activities in the developed countries of the world. We can already see the potential dangers in our increasingly rigorous search procedures against hijacking. Such measures carried to extremes would not only make modern life impossible but would destroy the basic value system of the Western world.

Mankind's survival now depends upon the development of compassion and mutual concern. Those who argue that man's basic action pattern is violence are, in today's conditions, concluding that we cannot adapt to the necessities created by our new powers of destruction and communication.

We cannot be certain that mankind will succeed in changing the characteristics he has inherited from his genetic and cultural past. We can, however, be sure that failure to adapt to the new realities we have ourselves created will be fatal.

We must search for synergies, ways in which all parties to disputes can be better off following negotiations. We are gaining societal skills in this area far more rapidly than we have so far realized; the time has come for us to concentrate national and international attention on this urgent requirement.

This is not a proposal for instant Utopia. Pain and grief and fear and anger will remain. Man's survival, however, requires that he learn to understand and modify the patterns he has inherited so that they become compatible with the world he has created for himself.

8 The Shrinking Northeast

I don't agree with the assumption that one can change the system from the inside. To think that you're going to change a foreign policy that's based on the interest of the ruling class in a society by working for the State Department, and to think that these foreign policies don't have a political basis as well as an economic or class basis, is crazy.

Mark Rudd

As the choice between win-lose and win-win models becomes clearer, and as the infeasibility of violence becomes more obvious, the urban Northeast shrinks in upon itself. Fewer and fewer people want to admit that they belong to the mind-set which activates New York and Washington. This December 1973 article examines the potential for leadership from other parts of the country.

It has been about ten years since I started traveling around the United States as a speaker and consultant. During this time I have spoken in all but three states and have had an opportunity to examine both basic and changing attitudes in various parts of the country.

When I first traveled outside the Northeast in the

early sixties, it was clear that the rest of the country suffered from a serious inferiority complex. Everybody wanted to be seen as part of the Northeast, then considered as a rectangle between the cities of Boston, Chicago, St. Louis, and Washington. Those areas of the U.S. which were excluded by geography tried to compensate by adopting most of their new attitudes from those who lived or worked in the Northeast.

One of the superficial, but significant indicators of an area's mind-set is its attitude toward climate. Large parts of the United States have intolerable summer climates. The pattern in other areas of the world is to adapt to reality by working in the early morning or late evening. But in the American Southwest, for example, the normal working day is nine-to-five, even though working in the early morning would lead to far more effective communication with the rest of the country because of time-zone differences which can reach up to three hours.

Until recently, few believed that the non-Northeasterner's attitude of inferiority would change at any time in the foreseeable future. However, it now seems, partly because of negative events in the Northeast and partly because of positive events elsewhere, that the situation is changing rapidly. The characteristic which the historian Arnold Toynbee has claimed to be true of all periods of major change is emerging: We are finding that those areas which have been most successful in the industrial era are failing to change, while those which lagged behind are now developing patterns of leadership for the communications era.

Obviously changes of this type do not develop overnight; it is only as one looks back over a period of years that it is possible to see evidence of the shift.

For myself, I can recall two events which even at the time seemed clearly related to regional and national changes of attitudes.

In June of 1969 I was present at a conference called by Governor Daniel Evans of Washington State to discuss appropriate future directions for the Northwest area. The primary theme which emerged was that it was possible for the Northwest to avoid the effects of the negative initiatives which had developed elsewhere during the industrial era; the implication was that the time had come to chart an alternative course. Such a theme, which would have been unacceptable earlier, was at this conference common ground for many delegates and speakers and has since become central to thought patterns in this area of the country.

In July of 1973 I had the opportunity to talk to the Midwest governors and suggest that it was time for them to play a leading role in national dynamics. They decided that they would search for ways in which they could work within Bicentennial possibilities to open up a debate on the direction which America ought to take during its third century.

What are the forces which lie behind this shift in self-image? First, there is the breakdown of confidence in the Northeast. Those in the Northeast who have been most certain of the validity of their directions are no longer willing to push for their proposals; those in other areas are no longer willing to listen.

Furthermore, throughout the country there is a growing question as to whether not only the institutions but also the styles of the Northeast are suitable to the solution of the problems we presently confront. An ever larger number of people are concerned that the scandals in Washington do not primarily represent a breakdown in personal morality but rather the failure of our present centralized system of organization and management.

One consequence of this development is that those in other areas who formerly wished to be seen as part of the Northeast now do not: the Northeast is "decreasing" in size. Parts of the country which would previously have identified themselves with the Northeast are now looking for new geographical groupings which will free them to develop their own ideas and their own styles.

In addition, there is a new dynamic emerging. Parts of the country which have not industrialized are suddenly finding themselves important to America's future because of their raw material riches or their agricultural potential. Just as the oil nations of the Arab world have seen their power increase dramatically with America's need to import oil, so the relative position of those states in America which are raw-material-rich or strong in agriculture has improved significantly in a short time.

Periods of history during which patterns of relative advantage change rapidly are always extraordinarily perilous for all involved. Reactions are now developing which could destroy the new styles, hopes, and values of those areas outside the Northeast. Industrial-age pressures, although diminishing, are still enormously powerful. But if the newly self-actualized states could find ways to use their skills and cultural patterns, they could create favorable dynamics for their own citizens and also for the nation.

What do these states have to offer? The resource which is of primary importance is not their agricultural or raw material riches. Rather it is a style which is less separated from reality by academic rhetoric or statistical legerdemain. Even more critically, it is a style which accepts the importance of the basic religious values which have long been out of fashion.

The Second Copernican Revolution

9

There is a dawning realization that more of the same policies, more patchwork, more tinkering will not bring us out of our present crisis state. All of us—public leaders as well as private citizens—are coming up against the wall. Can we get over the wall? Can we tunnel through? Can we get around it? Rather than panic, it would be wise to stand back and size up our predicament.

Allan J. Maceachen

This talk was drafted for what was announced as a major Smithsonian conference on education held in celebration of the 500th anniversary of the birth of Copernicus in April 1973. Only fifty people attended, symbolizing the breakdown in education which I discuss in this paper.

Naturally, those of us who spoke abandoned our formal presentations and dialogued with the small group. My frustrations were abundant because I very seldom take the time to write a formal presentation. Fortunately, this book provides an opportunity to get reactions to what I wrote.

Our educational system is obsolete. These words are chosen with care. I am not arguing that our present educational patterns are obsolescent and in need of urgent change; rather I am stating that our educational system is designed to prepare our children for a world which no longer exists.

I am aware, of course, that this argument has been made so many times that it has apparently lost its power to shock and even more importantly, to move people to action. I hope to present some of the arguments in a sufficiently different context so that we shall rediscover together the extraordinary urgency of our situation and the magnitude of the steps which we must soon take if our children are to live successfully in a world which we have created.

It is my thesis that we have undergone a second Copernican Revolution which has changed forever the way in which man must perceive himself and the world in which he lives. This second Copernican revolution developed with the work of Einstein, Heisenberg, Bohr, and others who destroyed the static certainties of Newtonian physics and created a fluid interdependent world.

Unfortunately, this new model of the universe has not yet been understood either by those who theorize about our society or by those who control it. The educators, the politicians, those in the media, and the bureaucrats continue to think and act on the basis of the now discredited physical science models of the nineteenth century.

I suggest to you that many of our societal failures result from the fact that we are working with an obsolete scientific paradigm — that our perceptions are biased so that we cannot clearly see the truly critical issues of today.

This language and approach were developed by Thomas Kuhn in his book *The Structure of Scientific Revolutions.* Kuhn used the term "dominant paradigm" to refer to the basic way of perceiving, thinking, and doing which is associated with a particular vision of reality. A true revolution occurs when the paradigm being used by a society is no longer believed by the society to explain the range of phenomena which are of interest to it. The discoveries of Copernicus were prime movers in the shift from one paradigm to another as we moved into the industrial era. We are now undergoing another, far more rapid shift.

There is a deep danger which has not been understood by many of those who are arguing the reality of this shift in paradigms. The culture by which each society lives develops out of its dominant knowledge paradigm. In the past, when fundamental change has occurred in the knowledge paradigm, this process has destroyed the culture. This was the key understanding achieved by the British historian Arnold Toynbee. He showed that when economic, technological, or social conditions changed sufficiently, the dominant paradigm was unable to adapt. As a result, cultures either collapsed because of their internal contradictions or were overwhelmed by external enemies.

We need not despair, however. Mankind *has* achieved new understandings of the nature of reality in the past; we are gathered here to celebrate one such shift in perception. But if we are to be successful this time we must recognize fully that *the conditions under which our shift must take place are dramatically new*. The destruction and communication revolutions of the last 35 years have tied the world together so closely that our past conflict patterns are no longer functional. It is impossible for some new nation or region to rise to power in a different part of the world by forcing its leadership on America and the West because the capacity for violent reprisal is too great. Nor can we hope that the West will tolerate slow erosion of its present power position unless it fundamentally understands the need for cooperative patterns in the communications era which we are entering.

We must therefore rise to a challenge which is without parallel in human history. We must change the dominant paradigm through which we have lived for so long and create a new style of culture suitable to our new scientific understandings. While this task will certainly be difficult, I do not believe that it is impossible, and shall suggest the reasons for this statement later. Before doing so, however, I must summarize the various paradigms which exist in Western thought at the present time.

The Positive Extrapolists

The dominant paradigm is, of course, the one which has brought us through the industrial revolution and produced man's unparalleled productive power; it continues to determine policy despite the fact that it is so longer relevant.

Herman Kahn is perhaps the most effective theorist today for this viewpoint. He argued that it is possible to provide everybody on earth with a good standard of living within a century, that there are no substantial management problems in the way of such an achievement, and that the concerns of ecologists about shortages of resources are nonsensical.

From Kahn's point of view we are living through an awkward period which will resolve itself in the not too distant future. He sees no evidence that there will be, or needs to be, fundamental change in any part of our economy, socioeconomy, or culture. He can be described as a positive extrapolist: He argues that trends can and will continue to move in essentially the same directions and the end results of these trends will be basically good.

It is impossible to state all the implications of Kahn's stand, but I want to emphasize one in particular. Our present patterns of management and control depend on the Weberian theory of bureaucracy: the belief that people are willing to serve as replaceable cogs in an efficient social machine. This approach led to the industrial-era system of education which effectively stifled individuality. I think it is already clear that such a system is neither attractive nor viable. We are moving toward a system of education which permits the diversity of individuals; as this process continues, the bureaucratic institutions on which Kahn relies to create wealth will no longer function. Indeed, the beginning of the processes of breakdown are already apparent.

The Negative Extrapolists

The positive extrapolists have long been challenged by those who feel that continued growth is infeasible. One of the best known of the negative extrapolists is Malthus, the clergyman of the early nineteenth century who stated the dangers of unlimited population increase.

The latest of the negative extrapolist groups is the Club of Rome whose book *The Limits to Growth* has caused discussions throughout the Western world. There is no doubt that this book has successfully challenged some of the more obvious flaws in the positive extrapolist model.

But there is a basic problem with the work of the negative extrapolists. This model of reality and pattern of thinking about the process of change is, despite appearances, fundamentally similar to that of the positive extrapolist. Those holding negative extrapolist views do not or cannot imagine a basic change in the way societies operate.

While this group clearly identifies the need for major rapid changes in political strategies and values, their paradigm still assumes that change must be achieved from the top down. Over time, therefore, negative extrapolists become a warped sort of positive extrapolist. They move from stating the depth of the crisis to suggesting that the problems they have identified could be solved *if only* their solutions were applied. However, as the public does not perceive the necessity for the steps they are proposing, they proceed to justify greater and greater concentration of power among decision-makers so that essential steps can be taken.

Arthur Koestler's novel, *The Call Girls,* is about this type of mentality — about the experts who believe that they have a right to peddle their inhuman solutions to our problems. The mind-set from which this group works is well set out in the following quotation from his book: "We are a horrible race, living in horrible times. Perhaps we should have the courage to think of horrible remedies."

Although it is not obvious at first sight, positive and negative extrapolists use the same basic paradigm. It is this reality which explains one of the more extraordinary paradoxes of today: Those who are most negative about our present situation nevertheless believe that the institutional structures which brought us to our present point of crisis can still pull us out of our increasingly serious situation.

The Romantics

A second paradigm now operating in our society is intellectually less well developed. It is essentially the antithesis to the extrapolist paradigm which claimed that man could dominate natural forces. It has therefore always tended to define itself *as against* the extrapolist paradigm rather than in terms of itself.

Essentially this second paradigm states that the world will work most successfully if man is left fully free to define his own role — or, more colloquially, to do his own thing. The more extreme statements of this position argue that we have now reached the point from which man's Utopian goals could be achieved in the immediate future.

Those who put forward this paradigm are intolerant of *any* constraints. One of the most extreme holders of this view once informed me that there were no instincts in man — only learned behavior. He applied his theory specifically to the sex drive. He denied the persuasive work of those who show that man is a primate animal and that there are genetic patterns — as well as cultural history — which constrain our behavior and will continue to do so for as far into the future as we can see.

The attempt to realize the "romantic" paradigm dominated many of the communes of the sixties. It also affects the behavior of many young people at the present time. Their actions derive from the theorizing of Charles Reich in *The Greening of America* — and many others — who argued that the world would come together if each person did what he felt was important. It seems unlikely that this second paradigm will ever develop fully because we can already begin to define the basic fallacy in both the extrapolist and the romantic paradigms.

The Survival of Contradictory Paradigms

I recognize that the discussion so far must have seemed nonsensical to many. How can there possibly be two paradigms which claim to explain reality — let alone more. Why don't the "facts" determine what the paradigm ought to be. The eminent physicist Heisenberg has provided the answer by showing that we ourselves change the "facts" by actions and thinking.

What are the mechanisms by which paradigms survive even though they are not congruent with reality? There are two primary factors which ensure this result. First, there is the phenomenon of selective perception. Second, there is the phenomenon of self-fulfilling prophecy.

First, let us look at selective perception. The dominant paradigm of today argues that there are objective facts. However, the facts we perceive depend on our personal life history and the purpose for which we are observing the facts. It is impossible to perceive all the facts that exist in any situation — each one of us makes a different selection of the realities with which we are confronted.

Let us look at this hall and the people in it. A builder would perceive one set of realities, an architect another. An educator will be watching for one set of interaction patterns and a psychologist another. Young people will have one reaction to the composition of the audience, those who are older will see it another way. The limited number of those from the minorities, including the majority/minority of women, will find one more proof of the nature of our society in the fact that most of the audience is white, middle class, middle-aged, and male.

If it is possible to understand different patterns *within this hall*, then it is obvious that each one of us will perceive startlingly varying realities when we try to make sense of the overwhelming rush of events now taking place in the outside world. People do structure reality in many ways. These different structurings can seem to be reliable guides to action because of the second phenomenon mentioned above, that of self-fulfilling prophecy.

For example, the way that we structure our welfare system depends on the defined nature of the problem and the patterns of human nature we believe we confront. But once we set up a welfare system it constrains those within it to behave on the basis of the patterns we have assumed. Our present system is based on the belief that people will not work unless they are forced to do so. It is unreasonable therefore to be surprised when we discover that people adapt to this system.

Reality can indeed be made to conform to man's perceptions for a period of time. But this period is not unlimited. The end result of working within a faulty paradigm is the death of the culture which continues to use that faulty paradigm.

One of the realities which we must urgently understand is that there is no way to act effectively together if one does not share the same paradigm. World society is being torn apart by the conflicts resulting from the existence of different paradigms designed to explain the same reality. We shall either discover and come to share an appropriate paradigm for the interdependent world socio-economy which man has himself created or we shall destroy ourselves as we continue to use obsolete paradigms to determine our structuring of reality.

What is the New Paradigm?

Do we as a society have knowledge of the required new paradigm? It is my contention that the new paradigm exists and only needs to be catalyzed in order to become visible. Many people have worked to discover the way of looking at reality which is appropriate now, and we are at the point where this knowledge could be organized if society would commit itself to the task.

What justifications do I have for this statement? I only have time to cite two here. One reason for my belief is that an increasing number of people at the leading edges of their subject find it easier to talk to people on the leading edges of other subjects than to those in the discipline from which their own thinking grew. The thought leaders are struggling toward an understanding of the new paradigm while the disciplines are entrapped in the old paradigm.

The second reason for this statement is that the required new paradigm has existed throughout the nineteenth and twentieth centuries, but those who struggled to define it were largely ignored. Blake's insights are increasingly known. Let me therefore quote from Goethe when he met Schiller at a meeting: "Schiller remarked that such a dissecting method of dealing with nature could not possibly attract the layman. I replied that this manner may be uncanny even to the initiates, and that perhaps there was still the possibility of another method, one which would not tackle nature by merely dissecting and particularizing, but show her at work and alive, *manifesting herself in her wholeness in every single part of her being, from experience itself.*"

My topic is the implications of the new paradigm for education, and it would therefore not be appropriate to state at length the nature of the new paradigm. However, it is necessary to briefly set out the basic concepts.

We need to recognize that the discoveries of the physical scientists of the twentieth century are relevant to our patterns of societal organization. While their thinking has to some extent already influenced our theorizing about how we should manage firms and organizations, our understanding of societal patterns is still largely unchanged.

There appear to be three key patterns. First, we need to enlarge Einstein's discovery of the interrelationships between everything. Once we have perceived that everything is interrelated, we must then engage in the task of determining *which* interrelationships are crucial in each system in which we must act, and which can be ignored for the particular problem/possibility being considered.

Second, we need to enlarge Heisenberg's recognition that the observer inevitably changes the event he observes, and discover the implications of this thesis for human societies. Obviously, the effect of observation and reporting is more far-reaching in some cases than in others.

Third, we must consider the proven need for diversity in any viable system. We have become aware that reducing the number of organisms in an environment weakens its capacity to adapt, that the creation of single crops in large areas greatly increases the risk of disastrous ecological breakdown. We have not yet perceived the full implications of this insight for human society.

Some people find the realities of interdependence, uncertainty, and the need for diversity so obvious that they tend to forget that the assumptions of the disciplines are still those which existed before the breakthroughs of Heisenberg and Einstein and many others. I shall take my examples from economics because it is generally assumed to be the "most developed" of the social sciences. One of the key assumptions of economics, without which the discipline would fall, is its *ceteris paribus* assumption — the statement that one event can be examined in isolation. This violates completely the proved pattern of interdependence. Similarly, economics contains no theory of risk and uncertainty, and those economists such as Schumpeter and Ayres and Shackle who have dealt with this issue are held outside the mainstream of the discipline. Finally, economics works on the assumption that all men are motivated by profit maximization, thus ignoring the diversity of patterns by which mankind actually lives.

The Dilemma of Education

It is our past intolerance of diversity which is at the center of our educational problem at the present time. Our educational systems are designed in such a way that they reduce diversity. We have not yet found effective ways to change our educational system so that our increasing lip service to the idea of diversity is effectively translated into practice. This difficulty is seen most clearly in the continuing commitment of many policy-makers and idea-movers to bussing. This denies the right of communities to create their own forms of schooling and demands that children participate in an homogenized model of education. This type of education is designed to pass on the paradigm which is now dominant but which we have seen to be obsolete.

There is nothing new in a system of education which is designed to pass on the dominant paradigm. What is new is our growing recognition that the dominant paradigm is obsolete. We are therefore placed in an a-historical situation, for Western cultures have never deliberately created a fundamentally new system of education and socialization.

Our task is therefore extraordinarily difficult, for we have already seen that we are not talking about the inaccuracy of "facts" which have been used for decision-making purposes. We are confronted with the reality that the patterns we have used to structure information are themselves obsolete. Economics, sociology, political science, and the other social science disciplines are all based on the static, non-interconnected world of the nineteenth-century physical scientist who believed that it was possible to fragment knowledge into discrete parts without distorting reality. We now know that the whole is indeed greater than the parts and that we must study wholes to create valid knowledge.

In an attempt to deal with the failures of the disciplines, we have moved to a "problem orientation." Some institutions, often called think-tanks, deal with many problems. Others examine a specific problem and concentrate their effort, e.g., Center for Population Studies, Hunger Research Institute, War Control Planners.

But there are deep, indeed fatal, flaws in this approach. Each group must compete with others to gain support for their activity by trying to convince people and institutions that their project is more important than *any* other. Each group struggles to obtain the attention of the public and their dollars.

The result of this approach is therefore a cacophony of claims for priority attention. Many people are now fed up with hearing about our difficulties and are unwilling to listen to those who draw attention to old or new problems. Overwhelmed by data and unable to see any prospects for favorable change, more and more citizens are cutting themselves off from new information and denying hope for a better future.

Our problem-solving orientation is not effective in

educational terms. We must find another way of structuring knowledge if we are to be effective in introducing the idea of a new paradigm. Fortunately the groundwork for such a new approach has been laid. We are discovering that the only way to solve a problem is to change the way that people think about it: In other words, we redefine the problem into the new paradigm in such a way that the problem ceases to exist. The most remarkable statement of this approach is contained within John Platt's paper, "Hierarchical Reconstruction."

Let me give a couple of examples of the way in which this new approach functions. We declared a War on Poverty which has been less than successful because poverty is a necessary and integral part of an industrial-era society. We can only abolish poverty if we create new thinking about rights to resources in the context of a communications era.

Similarly, the continuing stress in international relations has brought calls for the strengthening of the United Nations. There has been little recognition that the patterns of organization of the nation state are themselves the problem and that they are central to the structuring of the United Nations. We can only move toward a peaceful world if we can discover a new concept of authority.

We need to create a new structure of knowledge within a problem/possibility mode. Effective education requires that the person has an unmet need — a problem — for otherwise he will not be truly interested in new knowledge. Nor will people have the energy for the action required to create change in values unless they are motivated by the existence of a problem. But the direction of this energy will only be useful if it is employed to change our perception of the situation from problem to opportunity.

The new frameworks in which we study might well be called problem/possibility nets. The two words "problem/possibility" recognize that we must balance current problems against future possibilities. The word "nets" symbolizes the fact that it is no longer necessary for people to be physically located in the same place. Instead they can use modern communication technologies to ensure their interlinkage.

Sufficient work has now been done in the creation of problem/possibility nets to make it clear that their methods of thinking/acting will be very different from the patterns used by those involved in disciplinary study or problem solving. We need to develop new styles for interaction and new formats for developing knowledge. The primary output of net is a p/p focuser which is used to assure that the most up-to-date information is available to students of the subject at various levels of difficulty and in print, audio, and video terms.

The Reasons for Hope

I stated earlier that I believed it possible to solve the problems which now confront us. Let me close by stating some of my reasons for this stand.

We confront an educational problem/possibility. We need to inform people that the way that they currently think and act is unsuitable to the conditions which mankind has itself created. Failure in this educational task will mean that we shall continue to move in the directions which we now know will destroy this planet; the only question is how long it will take before the process of destruction which has already started becomes irreversible.

We have seen that the first requirement for change to be possible is that people are aware of a problem —that they know that something is wrong. This situation exists. There is increasing cynicism about all the institutions which have the responsibility for solving society's problems.

The second step in solving a problem is to know how to turn the problem into a possibility. I have suggested with great brevity that the knowledge base already exists for this step and that only the commitment of the society is needed to develop this knowledge base into a consistent overall paradigm to support effective thinking and action.

If we are to succeed in our educational task, the third requirement is to have the time in which people can rethink their models of reality. This meeting is symbolic of our situation. People in our society do not have to spend all their lives in physical toil in order to create the goods and services they need for survival. The educational enterprise in this country provides the possibility to reach every person and to give everybody the chance to discover the changes which are developing in the world.

Indeed, it can be argued that discussion of the need for a change in paradigm is very urgently needed in the formal education system today. Our schools and colleges are reality-poor — today's conditions are little reflected in the classroom. This results not only in students being ill-prepared for the conditions they find in the outside world when they leave the educational process; it also ensures that they see the educational process as a chore which they endure because it is required by the society or because it will bring them a better job or for a dozen other reasons unrelated to the true excitement of good education.

Fourth, we are not restricted in our educational enterprise to the formal classroom setting. The media in all its forms have an unparalleled possibility of moving educational information to people. I am not suggesting, of course, that the present methods of moving information will be suitable for the task we now need to accomplish. The methods of the media, like those of all institutions, are of course derived from the paradigm of the industrial era. I am suggesting that the technology does exist to permit people to participate in creating new knowledge and discovering the future they desire for themselves. A few of the activities being developed by cable companies and video buffs show the potential we have in this area.

We do not live and never can live in a society of affluence where people can have all the resources which they want. But we are already moving into a society of abundance where it is necessary and possible to provide all people with those resources which they need to develop themselves and to help create a better society. We are creating a society of enoughness in which people will accept the principle that too much is just as destructive as too little.

We have a choice to make. If we continue our drive toward perfecting the industrial era society, we shall destroy this planet on which we live. If we understand that we are undergoing a change from the industrial era to the communications era that is as profound as the previous shift from the agricultural to the industrial era, then I am convinced that we can create a better society.

This better society will not be an Utopia, nor a Lotus Land. It will be a world requiring far greater responsibility from all of us, both to create it and to live in it. Thus, while I am convinced that we can create this new society, I am far from certain that we shall make the effort which is required in order to do so.

If I study our current situation logically, I must admit to a deep feeling of pessimism. But as we have seen, logical study can only exist within the industrial-era paradigm which is now outmoded. My personal subjective look at the future convinces me that we shall indeed act in the ways required to continue the history of mankind and to save this planet. But I remain aware that my personal subjective look is only relevant if we create dramatically new patterns of self-fulfilling prophecy.

The first Copernican Revolution was sparked by a very few men. The second Copernican Revolution will only be possible if very many of us act together to achieve it. I hope that we may join together in the search for the communications era paradigm and the types of societies which it will create.

10 Guaranteed Income vs. Guaranteed Jobs

We shall be able to rid ourselves of many of the pseudo-moral principles which have hag-ridden us for two hundred years, by which we have exalted some of the most distasteful of human qualities into the position of the highest virtues . . . All kinds of social customs and economic practices affecting the distribution of wealth and of economic rewards and penalties, which we now maintain at all costs, we shall then be free to discard.

John Maynard Keynes

Our society is organized around economic realities and one immediate shift which is therefore required is in our economic thinking. As our unemployment situation worsens, and as we learn that we are going to be short of conventional jobs for many years, we face an immediate choice.

Are we going to attempt to provide jobs by moving federal and state governments into a large-scale job creating role? Is government going to become the employer of last resort? Or alternatively, are we going to develop new forms of rights to income in this new situation?

This piece was published in 1973 in *Social Welfare: The Forensic Quarterly*, and was designed to help students debate these questions. It examines which of these two directions would be most likely to ensure the continuation of fundamental American values into America's third century. In it I use the term "guaranteed income" because it is now generally accepted; however, I do think that the term "Basic Economic Security" is both more descriptive and more appropriate.

The above quotation from John Maynard Keynes was written in the 1930s in a piece entitled "Economic Possibilities for our Grandchildren." Those of you who will be debating the topic of guaranteed income vs. guaranteed jobs are the grandchildren for whom John Maynard Keynes wrote.

Unlike today's economists, who use his name as justification for their policies, Keynes himself was well aware that we were living in a rapidly changing world. He knew that we should have to change our life-styles as we increased our productive powers. He would therefore be profoundly shocked at the attempts being made to preserve the patterns of the industrial era.

Mankind has to learn to deal with the new conditions which we have ourselves brought into existence by discovering how to alter the environment and the world in which we live. One of the primary areas in which we have to rethink our socio-economic patterns and our culture is in the relation between work and income.

Choosing the World You Want

It is this reality which places us in a new situation.

Normally, it is reasonable to assume that the solutions which have been used for social problems in the past will be suitable for the future. But this easy conclusion is denied us at this moment in history because we have changed so dramatically the conditions under which we all live.

In this debate we will be deciding, in a very real sense, the type of world in which we want to live. If we are to do this successfully, we must realize that we have absorbed — and been taught — the socioeconomic and cultural values of the industrial era. The patterns of thought we have inherited will tend to lead many of us to favor the option of guaranteeing a job over that of guaranteeing an income.

As you study the issue of work vs. income, you need to recognize that our current values are relatively new and contradict those which were proposed by Jefferson — one of the founders of the American Republic. Jefferson believed that it was impossible for men to be free if they did not personally control the resources required for them to survive. He proposed, therefore, that everybody should own enough land for them to raise crops to live in dignity. The guaranteed income is an updating of this idea in the context of today's world.

As the industrial era developed, however, we moved to new patterns. We discovered that people who owned land were unlikely to want to serve as the industrial workers required by manufacturing industries. We also discovered that people tended to earn as much money as they needed to live for a time and then to quit their work and return home. This led to problems of scheduling and an unreliable labor force. (These problems still plague the industrialization efforts of the developing countries.)

We therefore developed a new culture in which men were valued in terms of their ability and willingness to toil — the folk songs which glorified those who worked hard and long to build America come out of this tradition. We also introduced a culture in which families grew accustomed to the idea of an ever higher standard of living so that whatever a person earned it was never enough for what he desired. In the twentieth century, in particular, we developed the idea that a man's value is determined by what he earns.

Our present economic system reflects these values and would not operate successfully if we stopped believing in these values. In our society most people must gain their incomes by holding a job. This job provides them with the income that they need to buy goods and services. The demand for goods and services from those who hold jobs closes the circle and ensures that everybody can find the jobs they need.

Seen as a still picture, there appears to be no difficulty in continuing such an economy. Problems arise, however, when we realize that the industrial era has a tendency to increase productive efficiency on a continuing basis. Each year it is possible for the same labor force to produce more goods than they did the previous year using the same amount of effort. Another way to make this statement is to say that it is possible to produce as many goods as in the previous year with a *reduced* labor force.

So long as we, as a society, believe that we need more goods and services as our highest priority, this system works. But there has been a change in our values in recent years, and two forces are leading us to challenge the national priority on economic growth. First, people are coming to look at the quality of life available to them rather than the quantity of goods and services. Second, we are beginning to realize that we live on Spaceship Earth and that there is a limit to the amount of resources that we can use without destroying the planet on which we live.

At this point, the very economic patterns which

have served us so well operate as dangerous constraints. They limit our freedom to decide how to structure our society both in the rich countries and throughout the world. So long as we believe that the vast majority of households should be supported by somebody working, then it is essential that we provide jobs for all those who want them. In these circumstances, it is obviously immoral to fail to give a person a chance to earn a living.

But once we accept this pattern, we are locked into what Professor Gomberg has called "a whirling dervish economy dependent on compulsive consumption." Each year we must, as a society, consume more so that we can provide people with the jobs that they need in order to be able to buy the goods and services which can be produced by the more productive job-holder. This system cannot be changed so long as most people must earn their income by holding jobs. We are trapped in a system which destroys the freedom of people to work in ways of their own choice and which destroys the fragile ecology on which all life depends.

Some Basic Realities

There is much distortion — some of it deliberate —

in this area of discussion. Let us start with three basic realities from which all intelligent debate must start.

First, man's survival depends on the availability of a basic quantity of resources. If society's rules deprive him of these resources, he will die or will be hampered in developing his potential. The destruction of potential may be directly physical as when the malnourished young child loses his ability to learn, or it may be psychological following a continued loss of hope.

Second, man is a worker. It is necessary that man be provided with the opportunity to be active for otherwise he becomes self-destructive. Man did not develop as an idle animal, and there is now conclusive evidence that high living and lack of activity are bad for him.

Third, the ways in which man organizes his life and activities will necessarily vary with the conditions around him. There have been many styles of living in the past, and there will certainly be new forms of living in the future. Man's survival depends on his ability to take advantage of the new conditions that have been created.

The Reasons for Change

These three realities are not generally accepted by our society, and they would be hard points to make in debate. They are, however, the primary base for any argument which demands change in the present status quo in which it is assumed that everybody should hold a job.

The basic argument of those who see no reason for change is very simple. People should work in order to be entitled to eat. Any proposal for a guaranteed income is immoral because it promises them incomes without working.

Where do I, who believe strongly in the guaranteed income idea, part company with the argument above? I do not believe that people should be idle. But I do believe that the present socioeconomic system is *precisely* the factor which is responsible for idleness among a growing proportion of the population and the widespread tendency to assume that the employee is entitled to do as little as he can get away with.

Our present welfare system encourages idleness both by the way in which it treats people psychologically, and by the actual financial arrangements which exist within the various welfare programs. It saps and destroys the energy of the human beings who get caught in the welfare trap and are deprived of the opportunity to act creatively for themselves.

In addition, the necessity to provide jobs for everybody makes it impossible for us to demand performance. It is generally agreed among executives and engineers that it would be possible to fire some ten to twenty-five per cent of the working force of every firm without reducing efficiency. Our necessity to provide jobs for all who need them makes it impossible for us to demand efficiency because if we should do so we would increase the unemployment problem beyond our capacity to handle it..

The present structuring of our educational system is also related to the need for jobs to be available for all. Although we know that much of education today is not relevant to the world in which we live, we have created a myth that educational achievement and the ability to perform a job are intricately linked. This myth has enabled us to keep millions of young people in school and college, thus reducing the number of job seekers and helping to keep the unemployment problem under control.

Man has created machines which in many ways are

more efficient than he is. At the present time, our society still demands that man compete with machines. Instead of taking advantage of the potentials that we have created, we are denying the freedom to develop ourselves to the fullest and to discover what the destiny of the human race may be as we are freed from repetitive drudgery and gain the opportunity to create new life-styles.

Freedom and the Guaranteed Income

What then do the proponents of a guaranteed income hope to achieve through the adoption of their ideas? They argue that man is a striving animal who reacts favorably to freedom instead of constraint. Along with one school of humanistic psychologists, they agree that man rises to challenge as his basic needs for food, clothing, and shelter are satisfied.

In the industrial era it made "sense" for man to be deprived of freedom because his labor was necessary to the raising of the standard of living which was an agreed societal goal. Today, this is no longer necessary nor is it desirable. We have reached the stage which was promised to us by Aristotle who argued that it was impossible to abolish slavery until the looms weaved themselves and the lyres played themselves. Now we have automated work and we can provide people with the freedom to discover themselves.

Will people use this freedom intelligently? There is no easy answer to this question because we are asking it of ourselves. Can *you* personally learn to handle the freedom to determine the shape of your own life? If you and I cannot, then we certainly should not introduce a guaranteed income. But I would suggest to you that if this is truly our situation, then we have reached the end of the line of human development.

Man has taken over control of the evolution of his universe. If we cannot even control our own lives, is it likely that we shall be able to make the right decisions for the survival of the planet?

More and more thinkers are agreed that we need a sharp change in the way that human beings think about themselves and the way that they live — it has been suggested in particular that we need a "compassionate revolution." You are the generation who will decide what sort of society you want to create. One of your first choices is whether you want to create a guaranteed job program or a guaranteed income program.

Which Future?

One of the tools which futurists use in thinking is the scenario. It tries to set out the results which will follow if we move in certain directions. Let us look briefly at what may happen if we guarantee jobs and if we guarantee incomes.

Those who argue that we should create a guaranteed job program believe that society has an obligation to provide jobs for all who cannot find them within the normal patterns of activities. They therefore suggest that the government should act as the employer of last resort, providing jobs for those who cannot find employment elsewhere.

Those who make this suggestion are thinking within the pattern of the Depression thirties when there were many people without jobs because people were unable to buy all the goods which could be produced. Many — most — of those in the ranks of the unemployed had skills which would have been useful *if* people had had the money to buy the goods and services which could have been produced. It was therefore possible to find meaningful activity for the unemployed.

Today conditions are very different. Those who have

skills and intelligence generally have no difficulty in finding jobs. The problem is that an increasing number of people do not have the education, the skills, or the motivation to hold a job. The proposal for the government to guarantee a job therefore has a totally different nature from that which is generally assumed. In effect, the government is being asked to provide activity for all those who are unskilled, uneducated, and unmotivated.

What meaningful activity will government bureaucrats find for this group? The answer is only too obvious: There will be *no* meaningful activities. As a result, the lack of skills and education and motivation will combine with frustration to lead to endless problems of absenteeism and goofing off. What then?

The government will certainly become angry with those who are benefitting from the program and with those running it. They will demand stricter rules for people who are within the program. For example, one might imagine that nobody would be allowed to change his guaranteed job more than once every six months. In addition, people might be docked a day's pay if they were late for work.

There is a short word for this sort of system — it is slavery. If you think that I exaggerate, look at the trends in welfare practices in your state and neighboring states and discover the practices which are developing as we become unwilling to look after those on welfare. You can get a fuller picture of the results which will occur if we move in this direction by reading *Player Piano* by Kurt Vonnegut. You can also get a sense of the problems and possibilities by reading *I, Robot* by Isaac Asimov.

What then of the guaranteed income? We believe that we would see a flowering of imagination and initiative if people had the resources to act in the ways which seemed best to them.

We anticipate the organization of groups, which we have called consentives, where those living on the guaranteed income would get together to create the new styles of goods and services which we shall need in a world where consumption is not our primary goal.

We believe that we shall see the creation of diverse answers to social problems as people gain the freedom to experiment. For example, a group of Black mothers living on the guaranteed income in Harlem might join together to create new forms of day-care centers which are suitable to their needs and their culture rather than those which are presently being imposed bureaucratically out of Washington.

But we know that if we take this different course, which depends on trusting the imagination and creativity and responsibility of each one of us, it is impossible to predict too far into the future.

The subject of your debate seems at first sight to be comfortably limited. You are, however, dealing with the nature of man and the nature of the new reality of our society.

Your debates could possibly be one of the factors which would help us to discover the world in which we can/shall live. You do not have to see your debating purely as an extra curricula activity designed to provide you with brownie points in terms of admission to colleges, etc. You could perceive what you are doing as a way of influencing the thinking of your parents, your school, your community, about the way we ought to live. You have more power to affect people's thinking today than you realize.

11 Income Distribution and Social Change

Those who want to develop new leadership styles argue that the breakdown of our society comes from both the excessive concentration of decision-making power and the fact that authority is given to those who hold positions rather than to those who have the appropriate knowledge and competence. They see community involvement as opening up ways for competent people to become involved in decision-making.

Community Involvement
A Problem/Possibility Focuser

The emergence of the guaranteed income as a pragmatic political issue was one of the great surprises of the sixties. When the idea was first advanced in 1963 and 1964, it was agreed by almost everybody that it was totally unrealistic. By 1969, the idea had been espoused by President Nixon.

How did this change come about? Was it through the conventional political process? Or did a grass-roots commitment to the idea develop? This article, written in May 1973, discusses these questions.

During the 1960s the idea of a guaranteed income emerged from obscurity to become the heart of President Nixon's first term domestic program. Daniel Moynihan, who was deeply engaged in this pattern of events, has set out his view of what happened in *The Politics of a Guaranteed Income* (1973).

Moynihan places his comments in the largest possible context. He argues that the guaranteed income was "an extraordinary, discontinuous forward movement in social policy . . . in the very least promising of circumstances."

His overall claim is that the history of the guaranteed income "provides evidence that the American government is potentially capable of the 'fundamental social change' which is so much demanded by some groups, and for which I believe a persuasive case can be made."

If this claim is true — and I believe that it is — then those of us concerned with the process of social change should examine the events which led to this result with great care.

Daniel Moynihan asserts that there was a three-stage process. First, a number of academics developed powerful analyses of why existing welfare systems did not work. Second, President Nixon chose the unpopular option of a guaranteed income. Third, the intelligent PR approach adopted by the Administration changed the minds of so many Americans that the guaranteed income came close to being enacted as law.

This analysis reflects the reality model used by the eastern liberal establishment, which assumes that change is achieved from the top down.

There is an alternative view of social reality to which I subscribe. I learned it, in fact, while I was publicizing the idea of a guaranteed income in the early sixties. Testifying before a Senate Subcommittee of Employment and Manpower in 1963, I found great interest combined with total scepticism. I was told, "We're fascinated by the idea but it is not politically feasible." In effect, these politicians believed, as I do, that changes in public opinion must precede changes in policy.

At the start of the sixties, the public still accepted industrial-era values. There was general agreement that those who would not work should not eat.

What started the process of change in attitudes which eventually made possible Nixon's legislative proposals? To oversimplify drastically, there were two basic breakthroughs which led to public understanding of the need for a guaranteed income. Early in 1964, the Ad Hoc Committee on the Triple Revolution — automation, weaponry, and human rights — sent an unsolicited report to President Johnson in which it argued that America was just entering the third major transformation in man's history. It described the developing transformation as the movement from industry to communications.

Although the document was lengthy and complex, the press seized on its proposals for a guaranteed income with almost total unanimity. Coverage was widespread with front-page stories in many parts of the country. Editorial writers had a field day decrying promises of pie-in-the-sky. Controversy erupted around the sapping of America's moral fiber. Talk-show votes from the audience demonstrated the high percentages of negative feelings. The initial overwhelming opposition to the idea expressed itself vehemently.

The wave of public statements died away rapidly. After all an "Ad Hoc Committee" was just that, and a guaranteed income was "impossible"; why waste effort opposing this concept when other issues were more urgent?

But the concept had become a part of public debate; it is estimated that some ten million people read the document, and most Americans were aware of some media coverage. The idea of a guaranteed income was found useful — indeed indispensable — by a wide variety of groups. Public support, as shown in the polls, moved upward although most Americans continued to believe we should find jobs for all.

The second breakthrough occurred when, in the Government Commission on Automation report of 1966, the guaranteed income was seen as one of several possible solutions. By chance, the lukewarm recommendation for further study in the Commission report was translated by the headline writers of one of the wire services into full-scale acceptance of the idea. The guaranteed income thus became a permanent part of the work/income-distribution debate. After this date, any serious discussion of the welfare/unemployment problem had to include the guaranteed income proposal.

Extraordinarily, Moynihan begins his analysis of the process of "fundamental social change" *after* the process of alteration in attitudes was well under way. While his story does cover the "politics of a guaranteed income," it fails to examine the real factors which made possible the "discontinuous, forward leap in policy." Moynihan provides none of the information needed to replicate this process in other areas where profound change is also required.

Moynihan's failure of analysis was vitally linked with the failure to secure passage of the proposed legislation in 1970 and 1972. The Nixon Administration believed that it could afford to obscure the major reality which had caused it to propose the bill in the first place — the fact that a strategy keyed to the provision of jobs had failed to provide adequate incomes.

This choice of tactics eventually confused both legislators and the public. The painfully achieved gains in understanding of the total range of possible social changes surrounding the guaranteed income were almost totally lost by 1972. We became less aware of the realities of our automated era and the fact that we must create new relations between income, work, and employment.

The linked issues of poverty, activity, and a guaranteed income will not vanish because the President and the Congress failed to act in the last Presidential term. We are moving rapidly into a social system which creates an expanding outclass which lacks opportunity and/or skills to find roles in our complex technological world. Only creative policy-making can change present trends which threaten to become irreversible in the near future.

The Potential of the Bicentennial Era 12

I tried to save the Shire, and it has been saved, but not for me. It must often be so, Sam, when things are in danger, someone has to give them up, lose them, so that others may keep them.

Frodo, in the *Ring* trilogy by J. R. R. Tolkien

In July 1973, I was invited to the annual conference of midwestern governors. They wanted to examine the future and to learn what they could do to affect it.

The speech I gave was designed to create action. Much to the surprise of most of those present, the governors passed a resolution committing themselves to study the potential of the Bicentennial. Partly as a consequence of support generated by this action, some of the midwestern states are leaders in effective Bicentennial programs. (See, for example, the report from North Dakota in Part III of this book.)

I want to make four points in twenty minutes. Obviously, therefore, I shall use a large brush. There is a need for evidence and detail that I shall not be able to supply. Normally, indeed, I would have felt that there would be no chance of getting enough across to make a speech with this time limit worthwhile — I know, however, that you are used to condensed briefings and must ask you to perceive the next twenty minutes as a brief resume of an extraordinary mass of material which is now available on the shape of the future.

Here, then, are the four summary points.

First, the future is not what it used to be. It arrives more rapidly. It brings more change. It alters priorities in entirely unexpected ways.

Second, the future not only changes the world in which we live — it also alters the way in which our world can be effectively governed and managed. Effective government will require different styles in this new era we are now entering. As we shall see later, these styles are both old and new.

Third, it is peculiarly appropriate that this session be held for the governors of the midwest. Contrary to the accepted wisdom, this is one of the parts of America which is most capable of dealing with our emerging situation.

Fourth, the rapidly approaching Bicentennial Era of the United States, running from 1976-1991, challenges all of us to discover how Americans can be permitted to choose the future they want for their third century in the light of our changed realities.

Let me now take up each of these points in turn. First, we have become so accustomed to the onrush of change that we are unaware how startling developments really are unless we look backwards.

How are these changes affecting the basic priorities and goals toward which policies have been directed for decades? I believe that we are discovering that our most basic socioeconomic patterns need change.

What are some of these areas of basic change? One is that economic growth, which was assumed to be a panacea for all our problems, is increasingly the source of many of our most critical difficulties. We have made maximum rates of growth our primary goal to which all other requirements have been subordinated.

We need to rethink our situation in the light of our new realities. There is growing agreement that economic growth cannot be the primary priority in this country. We need to discover how to raise the quality of life. We should not stop growth, but we must make sure that it serves the needs of people. There is impressive evidence that a rise in the quantity of goods and services does not *necessarily* increase satisfaction.

Another area where we are being forced to change our thinking fundamentally is in education. Your problem, as governors, stems from the fact that the young people in your schools and colleges know that schools fail to teach about reality. People go to school and college because they must. What they learn in schools contradicts the realities they think they know from their own lives and from the television set.

The easiest reaction is to try to shore up the present system. But this solution avoids the critical problem. Our present education system is designed to teach children what our culture *already* knows. People will have no chance of surviving the torrent of change now being directed at them unless education comes to play an anticipatory role — unless it helps people to discover what could happen in the future as well as what *did* happen in the past.

A further area of change which has immediate, and profoundly difficult, policy implications is the changing definitions of health and sickness, life and death. Western man has been so impressed with the value of saving and lengthening life that he has given little thought to the quality of the life that is being saved.

This brings me to my second point. We usually think of change in terms of new technologies, new possibilities, new limitations. I have tried to show that the necessary consequence of change is an alteration in the goals for which we strive and the definitions of success which we use to determine whether what we are doing is worthwhile.

Let me quote from an editorial written by Jeanne Scott in the monthly trendletter *Futures Conditional*: "The meaning of the word 'success' is obviously undergoing change: it appears to be acquiring new aspects of cooperation, balance, evaluation made on the basis of multiple information, an avoidance of exploitation. It is perhaps already true that nobody is considered to have succeeded if they thereby cause others to fail in the long run."

There are some who argue that the idea of striving for success is itself obsolete. I believe that this view is naive. There is plentiful evidence that a species can only survive if it struggles to achieve. But I also believe that there is now clear evidence that the directions in which we strive and our models of success must change.

In particular, we must change our patterns of government. We are suffering through a failure of the *system* of government which we permitted to develop rather than the failure of certain men. Lord Acton was correct: "Power does tend to corrupt and absolute power corrupts absolutely."

This statement is a sober and irrefutable statement of fact. The mechanism which operates is that a subordinate, relating to a person who holds power over him, will consider what he needs to say to maintain or improve the relationship. The more unpredictable the superior's behavior and the greater his ability to affect the subordinate's life, the greater will be the effort made to please him. Patterns of communication are then determined by fear rather than by an attempt to provide the information which the superior, in reality, needs for effective decision-making in any situation. It is this situation which developed in Washington as we allowed decision-making power to be more and more concentrated. The results were inevitable and predictable.

It is of course far harder to find the solution than to define the problem. Indeed, there is still a danger that we may worsen our situation as a result of the present crisis rather than improve it. There may be a cry for truly incorruptible men and a search for the truly honest individual. Such a search is doomed to failure for the basic problem is not one of individual dishonesty or corruption but the malfunctioning of our system of government. Any person with power is cut off from some information — a person with total power gets no valid information at all.

How then can we govern? The "surprising" answer is that we can govern in terms of the ideals of the American constitution. Authority was granted by the American constitution; coercive power was not. Those in charge of the system were granted the right to act but not the right to deny liberty or life without due process.

We need to reinvent forms of democracy which are meaningful in the complex communications era that we have entered. The governance of America, and indeed, the world, depends on finding ways in which the citizen can be involved in decision-making about his own present and future.

This brings me to my third point. British historian Arnold Toynbee, has argued that change comes from areas of a country which have not participated fully in past successes.

If we apply this understanding to the present situation, it becomes clear that it will not be the Northeast which deals with the crisis which we presently confront. The Northeast still believes that the present patterns of government are viable and that Watergate was an aberration which can be corrected. They are not prepared to recognize the basic problem of our present pattern of government: the fact that the extraordinary concentration of power in Washington is itself the source of the breakdown.

We must therefore look elsewhere for commitment to change. We must work in those areas of the country which participated less in the industrial era and are therefore able to see its flaws more clearly. The midwest is one of these areas. In many senses it never moved out of the agricultural style. It may therefore be able to enter the communications era with little difficulty.

The agricultural era and the communications era share a basic characteristic: People must be aware of the consequences of their actions and be prepared to take responsibility for them. In the industrial era, on the other hand, institutions and organizations grew up which both disguised the responsibility one had for one's acts and, indeed, often made it impossible to discover the ways in which one could be effective.

There is much going on in this area of the country which could point the way to a more humane and attractive way of life for all of America's citizens and could also suggest new patterns for the world. But the effect of the efforts already being made here is diluted, if not destroyed, by the fact that some of the inhabitants of most states ouside the Northeast suffer from acute inferiority complexes. The inhabitants of most of these states believe that they cannot lead America.

I have made this point again and again as I have spoken across this country. There is no doubt in my mind about its validity, however uncomfortable it may be. Your states will not take the position of leadership which they could assume until they believe that they are capable of creating for themselves the new socioeconomic patterns which we so urgently need.

I have suggested so far that patterns of change in the United States, and indeed throughout the world, are now so dramatic that they require fundamentally new understandings. I have argued that these new understandings cannot be imposed from above but must be learned together by all interested citizens. I have argued that those states which have not participated fully in the benefits of the industrial era are most likely to ensure the changes which are necessary if mankind is to survive.

Obviously this challenge will test all the skill and resolution which exists in the United States. Indeed, an examination of the historical record shows that countries confronted with challenge of this magnitude have often collapsed. But I still believe that the challenge will be successfully met if those who have the capacity to act choose to do so.

I cannot agree with those who argue that mankind's doom is inevitable. But neither can I agree with those who argue that everything will come out all right anyway and that there is no need to do anything differently from the patterns of the past. I believe that we can manage or "govern" this change but only if we make the required effort.

Fortunately, we are at a moment in American history which is ideally suited to meeting our present challenge. We are rapidly approaching the Bicentennial of the American Revolution. Just as Americans rethought their situation in the years 1772-1776 and on into 1791, we must reexamine the problems and possibilities of our future.

I should like to take the time to tell you how people

can be given an opportunity to change their ideas in the light of new realities. The challenge I was given this morning does not permit me to concentrate on this area. However, I must make it clear that enough projects of this type have been carried through, particularly in this area of the country, to inform us of what must be done if people are to be able to learn how to choose the future they themselves desire.

I hope that each of you will decide that you need to help your citizens discover the possibilities of the future. I hope that you may decide that you need to cooperate, as a group, in such efforts for many of our present lines of communication ignore state boundaries. There are no patented answers to the type of program you should develop. But there is one key requirement — that of people participation. This will not be easy; indeed, it never has been easy. But democracy and freedom rest in the long run on the existence of an informed and active electorate which will take the time and make the effort to decide what sort of community, country, and world it wishes to live in.

I am profoundly convinced that we have reached the time where the basic ideals expressed in the Declaration of Independence are not only desirable but are also necessary to our survival. Few, I believe, would deny that we have moved far away from these ideals in this century. I believe that the challenge of the next few years is to discover whether we can regain the vigor and beliefs of the founding fathers. I am convinced that your states can play a key role in the necessary dynamics.

I am no mindless optimist. The potential for your leadership exists. But potentials are only translated into action by courage and wisdom. In the light of our present situation and attitudes, I hope that this meeting will lead you to accept the challenge to mold a more humane future.

13 Creating Myth for the Communications Era

We are as Gods and may as well get good at it.
Whole Earth Catalogue

While the midwestern governors did pass a resolution expressing the need for Bicentennial activity, those of us involved in trying to implement the resolution never succeeded in creating an overall action model for the midwestern states. I therefore became deeply concerned with our failure to take advantage of available possibilities and wondered why we had failed to do so.

The following March 1974 editorial from *Futures Conditional* explores the shift in patterns of leadership in our communications era and challenges many of our assumptions about who our new leaders should be. We need to begin to understand "leaders as servants" rather than as "men on white horses."

One of the less understood trends in our culture is the "death of the hero." When asked about their heroes, people of all ages give the names of historical people or fictional characters and children frequently relate to comic book figures. Very few present leaders have caught the popular imagination to a point where they are seen as outside the common mold.

Most of those who comment on this development seem to believe that the times are hard on heroes.

They argue that everybody has feet of clay and that we are no longer willing to acclaim other human beings.

There is, of course, much truth in this statement, but it is nevertheless too simplistic. Winston Churchill was certainly a hero, but he was multidimensional and far from perfect. The Greek gods were heroes, despite the fact that they were all too "human" in their sins. Joan of Arc was a heroine despite all her weaknesses, and her image could be employed by Charles de Gaulle in order to reinspire modern France.

As recently as World War II, it was possible for a great national leader such as Franklin Roosevelt to embody the will of the Americans for national victory. As recently as the 1960s, John F. Kennedy could state effectively the belief of the United States that it possessed something special in its form of government and thus inspire its people to want to help other nations. And as recently as the late sixties, the drive for economic growth and scientific mastery provided goals that leaders could use to motivate individuals and the total culture.

In the 1970s, however, the goals of total victory, national sovereignty, economic growth, scientific mastery, and all our other industrial era dreams are tarnished. Victory is known to be no longer possible in major wars, for it can only be bought at an unacceptable price in world destruction; indeed, even local wars increasingly end in stalemate because of the fears of major-power involvement. The belief of the United States in its own culture has been gravely damaged by Watergate and other national failures; other nation states are also losing faith in themselves. The drive for economic growth and scientific mastery are challenged as never before by the continuing strength of the ecological movement.

Few new goals have emerged to take the place of those which existed in the industrial era and which no longer demand allegiance. There is, of course, a thrust toward ecological balance, but there are so many views of the nature of this requirement that it does not provide a possibility for national leadership at this time.

Leadership essentially occurs when an individual is seen to embody and make manifest the needs of a culture at a particular time. S/He can only do this if s/he moves with the stream of the culture, if s/he makes visible the drives and dreams of a period, if s/he perceives the myths which inspire a culture. Once we understand this we can see why there are no contemporary heroes. Our cultures are so fragmented that there is no overall stream, no set of beliefs or myths which inspire a whole culture or even a major part of it.

What then do we mean by myth? The word symbolizes the fact that any individual's view of reality is partial. It is the myth of the culture which determines which parts of the total universe are seen by people as important, which are seen as unimportant, and which are essentially "invisible." A culture which loses the myth on which it is based, without replacing it with a new one, will necessarily die. This is the position of America — and indeed of the world — at this time.

Many people, of course, object to the very idea of myth. They argue that there is an objective truth and that man's progress is measured in terms of his ability to discover this objective truth. They argue that discussion about myth, with its necessary acceptance of the role of subjectivity, destroys the progress which man has made during the industrial era.

The difference about the nature of the way in which the world is structured underlies all our arguments today. Our disagreements, however superficial they may seem, usually involve deep philosophical questions. The fact that we cannot agree as to whether the energy crisis is real or unreal, was created by the oil companies, or is a warning of the real shortage of raw materials, reflects not only different perceptions of the "facts," but different perceptions of the way in which the world operates and reality is created.

Because people disagree so fundamentally, the public is now totally confused. The careful reader of the newspaper, or watcher of television, discovers that totally contradictory arguments can be made conclusively — a least in the opinion of the person presenting the case.

The disagreements about the proper course of action reflect our present disagreements about the proper role of leadership. Those who believe that we can do without leadership ignore the fact that effective leadership is necessary to perceive the needs of the times, to focus them, and to move people to accomplish the tasks and roles necessary to achieve these needs. Leadership is required to create a myth which will make the survival of the world possible: Only a world myth is viable in our closely interconnected society.

Such a world myth cannot be monolithic. One of the

primary ingredients of the communications-era myth will necessarily be a belief in personal and community diversity. We must learn to accept the right of people to be who they are and to live in ways which maximize their own personal potentials.

How can we create new myths? The first step in examining this subject is to recognize that we are undertaking a task which has never been rapidly achieved in human history before. We have first to understand the process of myth-creation and then implement it on a worldwide basis.

And so, what are the steps which we must take to create new myths.

New ideas for the shape of the communications era are being developed and presented. Each of these new ideas is the possible foundation for a new myth. What we now need to do is let the society perceive the variety of possibilities which have been discovered and to arrange for discussion.

What standards should we have for good discussion? Today we would normally argue that the issue which must be resolved is whether an idea/myth is feasible. But we are now discovering that the feasibility of an idea depends not only on present realities but also on the new realities that can be brought into being if people become committed to an idea or a process. We cannot decide that an idea is feasible simply in terms of what can be done today. We must also discover what new forces can be created to make an idea feasible.

The primary forces which operate to create reality are "self-fulfilling prophecies" and "self-denying prophecies." In the first case people decide that they wish to accomplish something, and they work together to achieve this result. In the second case, they perceive a danger which they wish to avoid, and they band together to avoid it. If we are to create myth, we must provide people with more complete views about the range of possibilities inherent in our situation so that they can strive to achieve directions which appear good to them and to avoid ideas which appear unsatisfactory.

Those who wish to be mythmakers will inevitably live in different ways from those who believe that it is possible to discover objective truth. The search for mythmaking techniques both requires, and will create, a new universe in which we shall perceive and value profoundly different patterns than we do at present.

14 Past, Present, and Future

We are challenged to break the obsolete social and economic systems which divide our world between the overprivileged and underprivileged. All of us, whether governmental leader or protester, businessman or worker, professor or student share a common guilt. We have failed to discover how the necessary changes in our ideas and our social structures can be made. Each of us, therefore, through our ineffectiveness and our lack of responsible awareness, causes the suffering around the world.

A Call to Celebration

This speech was written for the meeting of UPI Editors and Publishers on October 3, 1972, just before the Presidential election of that year. It suggests the ways in which our understandings of the past and the future can be meshed in the present to create a new society.

The fears which I stated about the Bicentennial have, unfortunately, come true. However, the potential of the Bicentennial to move people to reflection and action remains; the only question is whether we shall take advantage of this potential or not.

Just at the time that I completed this book, I had the opportunity to work in Richfield, a suburb of Minneapolis which is composed of so-called middle Americans. There is a widespread belief that people of this background are not willing to look at tough new issues. My experience during three days of lectures and seminars confirmed what I already believed: that the types of concerns raised in this book are precisely those which people want to have an opportunity to examine.

Past, Present, and Future

Given the negative attitudes which have already developed around the Bicentennial, there are an increasing number of people who feel that the next years should be expunged from the calendar. However attractive the idea may be, I believe it is beyond the state of the art! The Bicentennial must be supported — however difficult this may be — for it is the only currently visible way to demonstrate the problems and possibilities which lie before the American people, and by extension, the people of the world.

The years from 1972 to 1976 will be as crucial for the long-run development of the world as the years from 1772 to 1776 were for the future of America. In addition, 1976 opens the final quarter century before the year 2000, a period which will inevitably be a time for intensive rethinking of mankind's hopes and dreams.

I do not believe that the Bicentennial is beyond saving, although I know that the task will be extraordinarily difficult. Fortunately, the threefold division for the work of the Bicentennial Commission permits us to raise all the critical issues required to bring about basic change. The Commission has challenged us to reexamine the past, to dream about the future, and to plan in the present for the change from the past to the future.

Such a pattern is known to be crucial whenever people or groups wish to alter the direction of their lives or their organizations. They must examine first the forces which brought them to their present situation. They must develop a dream providing new directions which they are willing to work to achieve. Finally, they must discover evolutionary means by which existing trends can be redirected to create the different future they want.

Given this reality, how can we rethink our past, future, and present to permit ourselves to make the urgently needed change?

The Past: Re-Cast the Melting Pot

Up to the present time, countries have celebrated the battles which they have won and mythologized the battles which they lost. But the battles, whether won or lost, must in the new context of the communications era be seen as evidence of information failure. They resulted from the fact that new ideas caused conflict which was unsuccessfully resolved, thus making violence inevitable.

We should mourn all those who died, not only those on the winning side. We must also consider the ideas which they were willing to die for, to consider the dreams which made death more valuable than life. Battles have settled nothing, whether they be those between the Indian and the white man or between Americans and British. America did not even succeed in keeping the British out. You may have chased my Tory ancestors out of New York during the revolution, but I "invaded" Manhattan with no difficulty at all nearly two hundred years later!

The Bicentennial should be the time for reconsidering the ideas, the dreams, and the arts which are the heritage of different American ethnic groups. We need to see how the ideas of Indians and Poles and Chinese and Blacks and Italians and French and Chicanos and Anglos and Jews and all other ethnic groups can be woven into a multi-colored, brilliant pattern which together will be America. I find it deeply encouraging that Spokane's Expo '74 includes a Folklife Festival, focusing attention on the contributions of Americans from Africa, Scandinavia, Mexico, Japan, China, the British Isles, and those who were present when the rest of us came.

We now know that the melting pot concept for America was a mistake. We should never have tried to eliminate the cultural patterns of immigrants. Rather we should have tried to create synergies between different cultures to discover where and how the various cultures could enrich each other.

In the next years, each culture needs to rediscover its past and to perceive what it can bring to the Bicentennial, both in terms of its own self-renewal and the development of the greater whole. In fact, such a process is already developing and needs understanding and support.

The Blacks and Chicanos have led in the effort to rediscover their own identities. But one aspect which has all too often crept into these patterns must be avoided. No single ethnic tradition can be imposed on the whole culture. Rather, each group must aim to discover its own beliefs and then examine how they can be woven creatively into those of others.

It is now generally agreed by psychologists that the desire to dominate stems from insecurity. As ethnic groups become more sure of their own identity, they will be more willing to cooperate and less determined to dominate others.

The Future: Regional Dialogues

We start our attempts to bring about the needed changes in America with an advantage which is all too often undervalued. There is already fairly widespread recognition of the need for fundamental shifts in ideas and patterns if mankind is to survive.

There is therefore a willingness to consider various views of the future of man, to look again at ideologies which were previously fixed. In effect, people are willing to discover whether the ideals which were expressed in the Declaration of Independence are being effectively implemented by present policies.

I would like to suggest to you that the primary goal for the next four years must be to create a *world-wide* dialogue about the degree to which the ideals of the founding fathers are applicable to today's circumstances, and the ways in which they can be effectively implemented. We live in a world drawn together by communication: National boundaries are obsolescent just as state boundaries became obsolete early in the industrial era.

It is my personal belief that American ideals are more capable of introduction today than they were in the eighteenth century. Man's development of power over his environment makes the dreams of the founding fathers essential to the future of the world. This does not mean that I accept all of the formulations as appropriate to today. It does mean that only a real and true form of democracy can meet the challenges of the present and future. A tough-minded belief that mentally healthy human beings would rather grow than wither and would rather develop than decay is the minimal requirement for man's survival and success.

We need to enter into dialogue with the rest of the world about the patterns which would be effective in understanding American ideals, as opposed to present American policies. The West Coast and Hawaii could discuss with the Pacific community, the Southwest with Latin America, the South with Africa, the East Coast with Europe, the Northern tier of the United States with Canada and Alaska with the frozen North. These groupings would not be exclusive, of course, but they do recognize geographical realities.

In order to make possible this effort — and to symbolize it — we could launch three synchronous satellites to provide free communication for people-to-people dialogue throughout the world. In this way, we would show that any discussions about the future must necessarily be global in scope. The planet is now too small for discussion of purely national goals.

The Present: Change and People's Heads

If we are to reconsider the past and to create the future, people must be given opportunities to meet and plan together. They will require two types of information.

First, people need to be able to find out what is going on in their local areas, the activities which need to be carried out, and the opportunities for them to be involved. Second, they need to understand the massive forces which are presently changing the shape of the world and producing new problems and possibilities.

Many groups are working toward these ends. There are organizations in Hawaii and California and Maine which are working with state governments to perceive the effect of the future on their states. A TV station in New York has a continuing program to chronicle community efforts. There are small and large centers in cities and towns throughout the country which are trying to provide people with the information necessary for constructive action.

I believe that this move toward a new form of voluntary action is one of the more significant stories of today. These groups act on the assumption that communications rather than power is the primary source of change. The Bicentennial Commission has seen this reality and is working with many organizations — in particular women's groups — to enlarge this initiative so that every community can have the possibility of being involved in a reconsideration of its directions during the third century.

We need, during the next four years, to apply the knowledge we have already gained about the ways in which change in attitudes can develop. It is essential that we always remember that people change their minds because they see that there is another course of action which will be more favorable for them. Alterations in beliefs cannot be coerced.

The process of attitude modification requires three steps. First, people must be brought new information which is credible to them. Definitionally, a John

Bircher is not credible to a member of the Black Muslims and vice versa. One of the crises of our times emerges from the fact that the amount of information found to be credible by the population is declining continuously, and confidence in the statements of all institutions is dropping precipitously. We are in danger of creating a second tower of Babel where nobody can understand anybody else.

Second, people must be given the opportunity to discuss the information they have received. The fact that one is trusted to be as honest as possible does not mean that those listening will always agree with one's conclusions. People must have the opportunity to think through the issues which have been raised. Most people find it easier to do this in the context of a group of people with similar mind-sets.

Third, people must have the opportunity to act on their conclusions. It is the action which provokes feedback, and it is this feedback which permits people to discover where their conclusions are right and where they are wrong. Feedback starts the whole threefold process of discovery over again.

There are many ways to combine these three steps into effective programs. We know that it is possible to use the media for the input of credible information;

we know that it is possible to create small groups for discussion by working through voluntary organizations; we know that it is possible to find meaningful action possibilities for groups. If we should resolve to use our resources and our knowledge creatively, it would be possible for all of America to reconsider its values during the next years. The models exist. The necessary technologies exist. All that is lacking is the will.

15 Creating the Future

We have got to find ways together to look at the total individual, the individual's total capacity to pursue happiness, and the only way we are going to do this is to understand what the individual is supposed to be doing in each stage of his life and what are the things that are barriers to the individual's hopes and desires.

The final piece in this section was written as this book was being completed. It was designed to help members of the American Association of University Women, who, during the period from 1975 to 1977, will try to understand the way we should look at the future and to suggest directions in which we should move. In a sense, it summarizes the pieces that you have read so far.

In recent years, futurism has become one of the "in" fields for those who want to be trendy and chic. However, it is somewhat strange that we should suddenly have discovered the future because it is the place where we can confidently expect to spend the rest of our lives!

But what is the futurism? And how is it relevant to the average citizen? Or it it?

Those who try to answer these questions sometimes find themselves completely lost. There appear to be as many types of futurism as there are futurists, as much disagreement about the way to perceive the future as about the meaning of present economic trends.

There is only one way through this jungle and that is to understand that the arguments among futurists grow largely out of different assumptions about the nature of the universe and the nature of man. Futurism is one of the ways in which we argue about how things happen and how man can and ought to be involved in his society. For some authorities, futurism is just another discipline, for others it is an opportunity to reconsider fundamentally the assumptions about the nature of man and the universe.

There is a curious parallel to ecology here. For some, ecology has been a scholastic discipline; others have used it as an opportunity to open up questions which have not been taken seriously by our culture.

How then does one become a serious futurist? The answer I give here will undoubtedly differ from what other types of futurists would say, but I believe that the prime necessity is for one to be concerned about the future and to want to be involved in creating better directions.

From this point of view, many of the most used futurist techniques are either too complex or too tied up within present industrial-era patterns. For example, the Delphi technique, where experts are asked their opinion, tends to re-create the conventional wisdom rather than discover where fundamental breaks in trends are likely to occur. At the 1972 convention of the World Future Society, one speaker illustrated this point by stating what would happen under a normal Delphi if he asked how long the meeting was going to last. He said that most people would agree that the meeting would run for the scheduled time and that the person who stated that it would end in ten minutes would be ignored. However, he said the latter might be the person who knew there was a bomb in the room and that one should pay attention to him!

What sort of techniques might one use to get a better hold on the future? Each one of us needs to be more aware of the range of options that exists at the present time and which could come into existence depending on the directions in which we make our efforts as individuals and groups. In this brief paper there is only space to mention a few models which can be very helpful. One of them was invented by Ken Davis, who suggested that you try to write your autobiography for the next twenty years rather than the last twenty years. In trying this with students, he discovered that, despite the understanding of young people that the world could be expected to change drastically before the end of the century, they had not incorporated many of their new understandings into their own life plan.

A second technique which I find useful is to imagine the world as it might appear at some point in the future if things go badly and if things go well. At the beginning of the seventies, I prepared a pamphlet for the United Nations in which I set out a series of news stories that might be written in the year 1980. One set assumed that trends would continue without change and the other assumed that we would begin to make intelligent efforts to create a more human future. The depressing thing about this pamphlet is that all the bad trends are continuing to develop and there is little evidence of movement in more favorable directions.

But techniques are not really the primary need. These are available or can be developed; we prepared a number of them in the first two years of our trend-letter, *Futures Conditional*. It is much more important to develop frameworks and contexts in which the concerns and enthusiasms of citizens can be mobilized. It is my personal conviction that people are particularly ready at this time to act to create a more human future. Our failure as a society up to the present time has been to provide few opportunities for meaningful large-scale activity.

Following are a few recent frameworks which I bebelieve to be particularly hopeful:

Communities of '76. This program calls on communities of all sizes to consider how citizens can participate in creating a more human future. A number of models are being suggested which would allow people with different levels of concern and commitment to become significantly involved. One way of stating the idea of this program is that it is designed to give people a chance to perceive the most fundamental questions for their communities during America's third century.

Classes of '76. This program is designed to reconsider the nature of education at a time when it is clear that the assumption that the old know and the young must learn is no longer tenable. In light of some of the arguments of the sixties, it is perhaps necessary to state that I am not arguing that the young know and that the old must learn. Rather I am suggesting that we must somehow learn together what the new era which we are entering holds in store for all of us. It is suggested, therefore, that all educational establishments should consider what education should be and announce their findings, using all forms of communication, on commencement day or the last day of the semester. Specific models for this purpose have been developed.

Congregations of '76. It is sometimes forgotten that the churches played a major role in the revolution: They permitted people to feel that is was all right to fight against King George and for America. It would appear particularly appropriate that the churches play an important role in the Bicentennial era because there is growing evidence that if we are to survive the increasing interdependence of the globe we shall have to redevelop religious values. The American Lutheran Church has suggested that each congregation should reconsider its mission for America's third century and rededicate itself on Sunday, July 4. Other denominations may want to consider the possibility.

These programs differ from the types usually proposed because they do not contain highly specific, detailed models. Rather, they are designed as "umbrellas" under which many groups with diverse concerns can work to achieve goals which, without widespread effort, might be impossible. It is in this connection that the use of the Bicentennial idea is valuable, for it makes it possible to break through patterns of inertia which might otherwise make it impossible for anything large-scale to happen. Indeed, the idea of a Bicentennial era, proposed by John D. Rockefeller III and others, promises to provide a continuing drive for fundamental change.

It is in this context that the topics which have been adopted by the AAUW have their full weight, for they clearly assume that it is possible for the future to be different from the past. They assume that we have the talent and the skills to change our directions when they are shown to be wrong.

The immediate crisis is, of course, in the relationship between economic change, ecological change, and the needs of the developing countries. More and more people are realizing that we have each consumed a greater share of the world's resources than is reasonable in the light of real conditions. More and more people are prepared to cut back on their levels of consumption both to save resources and to provide a fairer share of the world's wealth to others.

However, this highly desirable step can, unless it is accompanied by fundamental change in socioeconomic systems, actually worsen the position of everybody. Although there is no conclusive proof, I am personally inclined to believe that one of the factors which is deepening the recession at an unexpected pace is the change in the perceptions of people about their rights to consume. Unless we change our patterns of distributing resources at the same time as we change our consumption patterns, it seems clear that we shall bring about a world-wide depression, if not this year, then at some time in the relatively near future.

We need to read those few authors who have discussed the question of systemic change in economics and ecology. We need to recognize that neo-Keynesian economics locks us into a system in which more production requires more consumption requires more resource use to create more jobs which creates more production and thus round the circle. Our socioeconomic system is obsolete. Only profound change can break us out of the present situation where we can expect either double-digit inflation, or double-digit unemployment, or both.

Our economics have contributed to the development of a single-track system in which diversity was discouraged. Now as we begin to recognize that economics should not control the evolution of our societies, we are also beginning to learn that pluralism is not only desirable for the sake of variety but also essential for our survival. We are learning that a monoculture is as dangerous as a monocrop in our fields. Pluralism is the absolute necessity because it ensures a variety of points of view. Indeed, pluralism and creativity are closely meshed, for it is the mixing of unfamiliar points of view which results in new ideas and new directions.

Our society now continues to move toward the negative results which were brilliantly forecast by dystopian writers such as Huxley, Orwell, and Vonnegut. If we are to create a more human society, we shall have to learn that it is possible to invent new ideas and to find ways to move these ideas so that they affect people and cause them to act in new ways.

And this brings us full circle. The future is not determined. The directions in which we move are determined by self-fulfilling and self-denying prophecies; people strive to achieve goals that they consider worthwhile and they strive to avoid directions which they think would be damaging. We need to invent new ideas and directions which people will support and thereby create a more human world.

In effect, the future is created by inventing new "myths" which lead us to see the world in new ways. Our world, as it presently exists, is a reflection of our ideas and our beliefs. We can change our ideas and our beliefs and thus change the world in which we actually live. As Churchill said: "We shape our buildings and then they shape us."

Futurism, then, is the re-designing of the future: It is an art and not a science. If we have respect for the mystery of the creative process, then between us we can create a world which reflects our hopes rather than our fears.

At the time when *Alternative Future for America I* and *II*, the first two books in this series, were published, it was still unusual for people to believe that an alternative future for Americans was required. Both of these previous editions concentrated, therefore, on my own work. There was at that time no overall change process to which my work seemed closely related.

This is no longer the case. Throughout the country more and more people are aware of the need for new directions and of their capacity to help bring about the necessary change. This overall effort is being facilitated by the Northwest Regional Foundation, among others; this grouping grew out of the dynamics of Expo '74 in Spokane and its Environmental Symposium series.

The material which follows was developed primarily by the Northwest Regional Foundation to provide people with an overview of the theoretical and action possibilities which exist at the present time. It is drawn from an information service called *Futures Conditional* which is published ten times a year at a cost of $20.00. You are invited to write to the Northwest Regional Foundation, P.O. Box 5296, Spokane, WA 99205 for a sample copy or to subscribe if you should wish to do so. Some of you may have seen

Futures Conditional in its previous form when it was published by me. It was taken over by the Northwest Regional Foundation in January 1975 and is now published as a loose-leaf package.

Is one sense, this book is designed to introduce you to the possibility of action through involvement. It is not enough to read books if each of us is to attain the potentials which are open to us. We must find ways to act so that we can take advantage of the possibilities that personkind has opened for itself, while avoiding the dangers which presently exist.

A Call to Celebration 16

This document was created in 1967 by people of several countries; their names are not important for they have tried to express the spirit of an age. You may circulate any part of it in any form. It is meant to grow. You are challenged to improve words, paragraphs, change its form, translate it into music, poetry, pictures, tape . . . .

So others can share your vision, please send copies to:

A Call to Celebration
c/o Robert Theobald
P.O. Box 5296
Spokane, WA 99205

I
and many others
known
and unknown to me
call you:

• • • to celebrate our joint power to provide all beings with the food, clothing, and shelter they need to delight in living.

• • • to discover, together with us, what we must do to use mankind's unlimited power to create the humanity, the dignity, and the joyfulness of each one of us.

• • • to be responsibly aware of your personal ability to express your true feelings and to gather us together in their expression.

We can only live these changes. We cannot think our way to humanity. Every one of us, and every group with which we live and work, must become the model of the era which we desire to create. The many models which will develop should give each one of us an environment in which we can celebrate our potential, and discover the way into a more humane world.

We are challenged to break the obsolete social and economic systems which divide our world between the overprivileged and the underprivileged. All of us, whether governmental leader or critic, businessman or worker, professor or student, share a common guilt. We have failed to discover how the necessary changes in our ideals and our social structures can be made. Each of us, therefore, through our ineffectiveness and our lack of responsible awareness, causes the suffering around the world.

All of us are cripples — some physically, some mentally, some emotionally. We must, therefore, strive cooperatively to create the new world. There is no time left for destruction, for hatred, for anger. We must build in hope and joy and celebration. Let us cease to fight the structures of the industrial age. Let us rather seek the new era of adundance with self-chosen work and freedom to follow the drum of one's own heart. Let us recognize that a striving for self-realization, for poetry and play, is basic to man once his needs for food, clothing, and shelter have been met — that we will choose those areas of activity which will contribute to our own development and will be meaningful to our society.

But we must also recognize that our thrust toward self-realization is profoundly hampered by outmoded industrial-age structures. We are presently constrained and driven by the impact of man's ever-growing powers. Our existing systems force us to develop and accept any weaponry system which may be technologically possible. Our present systems force us to develop and accept any improvement in machinery, equipment, materials, and supplies which will increase production and lower costs. Our present systems force us to develop and accept advertising and consumer seduction.

In order to deceive the citizen into believing he controls his destiny, that morality informs decisions, and that technology is the servant rather than the driving force, it is necessary to distort information. The ideal of informing the public has given way to trying to convince the public that forced actions are actually desirable actions. Miscalculations in these increasingly complex rationalizations and the consequent scandal account for the increasing preoccupation with the honesty of both private and public decision-makers. It is, therefore, tempting to attack those holding roles as national leader, professor, student. But such attacks on individuals often disguise the real nature of the crisis we confront: The demonic nature of present systems which force humanity to consent to its own deepening self-destruction.

We can escape from these dehumanizing systems. The way ahead will be found by those who are unwilling to be constrained by existing forces and by our willingness to accept responsibility for the future.

Indeed the future has already entered the present. We each live in many times. The present of one is the past of another, and the future of yet another. We are called to live knowing and showing that the future exists, and that each one of us can call it in, when we are willing, to redress the balance of the past.

In the future we must end the use of coercive power and authority; the ability to demand action on the basis of one's hierarchical position. If any one phrase can sum up the nature of the new era, it is *the end of privilege and license.* Authority should emerge through a particular ability to advance a specific shared purpose. We must abandon our attempt to solve our problems through shifting power balances or attempting to create more efficient bureaucratic machines.

We call you to join man's race to maturity, to work with us in inventing the future. We believe that a human adventure is just beginning, that humankind has so far been restricted in developing its innovative and creative powers because it was overwhelmed by toil. Now we are free to be as human as we wish.

The celebration of our common humanity through joining together in the healing expression of one's relationships with others and one's growing acceptance of one's own nature and needs will clearly create major confrontations with existing values and systems.

The expanding dignity of each man and each human relationship must necessarily challenge existing systems.

The call is to live the future: Let us join together to celebrate our awareness that we can make our life today the shape of tomorrow's future.

17 Jonah/Irene Orgel

Those of us who were brought up within Christian homes were taught to perceive God as all-knowing. It followed from this perception that the evil in the world must necessarily be accepted, if not intended, by God. Such a conclusion has led to the loss of faith by many religious people as they were overcome by griefs too great to bear.

Irene Orgel's parable which follows suggests an alternative view of God. It suggests that "God" learns as humanity learns; that it is our own lack of knowledge of values which causes the evil in the world.

It would be naive to see this parable as the complete way of looking at God. But the vision which inspires this approach is closely related to the statement that the Holy Ghost is present when "two or three are gathered togther in his name." Alternatively, for those who prefer a secular metaphor, it argues that synergy is possible when people meet together within a cooperative style in order to create possibilities and/or to solve problems. Synergy, in this context, means that new knowledge is created through discussion.

Our first contact with this piece was as a mimeograph copy without any source reference. We have tried for several years, without success, to locate Irene Orgel, the author of the following parable. Do you know how to contact her? If so, please let us know.

JONAH

"I want to talk about Jonah," said the man on the psychoanalyst's couch.

"Jonah and the whale?" asked the doctor.

"Jonah," said the patient, "before he ever met the whale. Jonah, first of all when he was running away. Jonah, the man with the big fear pursuing him. When God looked for Jonah, he couldn't see him for the dust. When God called to Jonah, Jonah didn't hear him for the wind which was whistling in his ears.

Jonah ran to the end of the land, as far as he could go, and when he reached the end of the land and came to the edge of the sea, he took a boat.

"There's someone guilty on board," said the sailors when a storm arose.

"That's me," thought Jonah without a second thought. That's the sort of egotist he was. He didn't give a thought to all the crooks and smugglers on the passenger list. He didn't consider the cut-throats in the crew who had signed up to get away from the scene of their crimes. No, Jonah had this guiltier-than-thou attitude, and all that he could think of was Jonah.

He opened the door of his stateroom and he said: "Here I am, boys."

The sailors picked him up (he had asked for it) and

swung him by his arms and legs, one, two, three, and yo-heave-ho, and over he went. Splash! And into the jaws of the whale.

("The womb phantasy," murmured the analyst.)

"Well, whatever it was," continued the man on the couch, "in ventro and de profundis" Jonah cried out to the Lord. And this time Jonah's words weren't the panting incoherent snatches of a man running away from his Fear. This time it was despair; but it was his own despair. And for the first time he cried out with his own voice.

In the belly of the whale, Jonah was transformed. He reversed all his behavior patterns. It was like a religious experience. What am I talking about! It was a religious experience. He was the prophet Jonah, wasn't he? People who had known Jonah before, and met him after the whale, said:

"Jonah, you're a changed man."

It wasn't that his hair had turned white or anything like that. It was simply that everything he had done before, he now did in reverse. He had been a fearful man and he had suddenly changed into an angry man. As precipitately as he'd run away from Nineveh, he now wanted to dash toward it. Just as sharply as he'd turned away from God's word, he now wanted to overdo God's word.

"Hey, son!" shouted God.

"I'm off to Nineveh," yelled Jonah. "Don't stop me."

"Wait a minute," said God, trying to keep up with him. "What are you going to do when you get there?"

"Fire a burst!" replied Jonah.

"Now take it easy," said the Lord, and he held Jonah back by his shirttail.

"But they don't listen to YOUR WORD," stormed Jonah, with his super-duper-super ego. "We're not going to stand for that, are we?"

So the Lord made him sit down and cool off under a gourd. Gurd or Goord, is it? I never said it out loud before. I never could see why the business about the gourd was stuck on the end of this story. Yet it's the logical ending. The gourd represents every living thing.

As if in a speeded-up documentary movie, Jonah

saw it sprout from seed, then flower and then, to his consternation, it withered before its time.

"What's the big idea?" he protested.

"Look," said the Lord. "Don't you go getting sentimental over the life and death of a gourd. This happens to be one of the stiffest, prickliest, least organized of all the organisms in my vegetable kingdom. Whereas people, and this includes even the people of Nineveh, are the most highly organized of all my organisms. Where's your sense of proportion, son?"

Then Jonah understood.

His fear and anger fell away from him like so much unnecessary luggage, jettisoned. And this left room for love of the whole of creation to well up in him. And he was no longer angry with Nineveh, which had after all represented nothing to him but his own past. Instead of a turreted town crammed with phantasmagoria, it now appeared before him as a plain, ordinary, workaday city, and the people in it were only people, after all.

Imagine Jonah now, having left behind his luggage of confusion and turmoil. Free-striding and life-accepting, as he walked along the road to Nineveh. Simplicity was in his pocket, and the principle of the gourd was deep-rooted in his heart.

Without knowing the scientific details, he knew he was a man who had come out of the sea. And he knew he was a man who had come out of the sun. The Lord had told him all this when he said: "Consider the gourd. Respect it."

Because Jonah thought things out best when he was walking, he had a long, calm discussion with the Lord on the way to Nineveh.

"If you created the seed and the life and the sprouting," Jonah asked, "why did you create the negating and rejecting? The fear and the anger and the running away?"

"To tell you the truth," said God, "I had no idea it was going to go this far. Of all the roads it might have taken, this is surely the most surprising. When I was in the infinitesimal speck which held the potentiality of creation, how was I to know it would expand, to become the universe? And when I blazed and exploded in the innumerable suns, how could I foresee that out of the near collision of two of them would leap the tide which would cool into planets? This, by the way," said God confidentially, "I learned from Sir

James Jeans. Most of what I know comes from Albert Einstein. Before that I had only Newton to go on. And before that . . ."

"But before Man," asked Jonah, shocked out of his wits, "do you mean you understood nothing at all? Didn't you exist?"

"Certainly," said God patiently. "I have told you how I exploded in the stars. Then I drifted for aeons in clouds of inchoate gas. As matter stabilized, I acquired the knowledge of valency. When matter cooled, I lay sleeping in the insentient rocks. After that I floated fecund in the unconscious seaweed upon the faces of the deep. Later I existed in the stretching paw of the tiger and the blinking eye of the owl. Each form of knowledge led to the more developed next. Organic matter led to sentience which led to consciousness which led inevitably to my divinity."

"And what will you become next?" asked Jonah.

"I don't know," said God reverently. "I am waiting to be told."

"By whom?" asked Jonah, and he looked around the lonely landscape in dismay.

"How I tremble," sang God, "in rapture before the next stroke of consciousness! How I yearn to be created further!"

"But I don't like this at all," cried Jonah. "Can't we go back to the way it used to be? You scared me to death most of the time. But how I loved to hear your scolding voice."

"I couldn't go on forever," said God severely, "telling tall stories about whales, any more than I could have remained inert once the first colloidal systems started to form or inchoate once the form of the atom was established."

"But it was cozy," sobbed Jonah. "You and me; I and thou."

"Now it shall be We are One."

"And shall I never call you father any more? And will I never hear you call me son again?" asked Jonah.

"You may call me," said God agreeably, "anything you please. Would you like to discuss semantics?"

So Jonah found himself alone on the road to Nineveh.

And yet he was not alone. For the gourd was with him, and the lungfish, and the stars. He knew that he was a man who had come out of the sea. And he knew that he was a man who had come out of the sun. And in Nineveh he took root, and he flowered in the expression of his consciousness until he died.

He married a Nineveh girl, of course. That goes without saying.

The man on the couch fell silent. After awhile he sat up and started to grope with his feet for his shoes on the floor. Then he bent over and slowly tied his shoelaces. Then he stood up.

"Well, I just wanted to talk about Jonah," he explained diffidently.

And then he bolted from the room.

18 How to Dialogue

This is the only piece included in this book which was also published in *An Alternative Future for America II.* It was originally written not only to point out that dialogue with others could have fruitful results but that the approaches to a dialogue session necessarily had to be profoundly different from those at committee meetings.

In the years since this piece was written we have come to understand more fully the dynamics required for effective dialogue. We are still not sufficiently aware, however, that we must behave very differently if we are to achieve *effective* dialogue. The brief extracts reprinted here state the "rules" which are necessary for synergy to occur.

People can only work together if they trust each other. The need to build trust is far greater now than ever before, for the degree of suspicion has risen dramatically since this piece was written. Time spent in getting to know each other is not wasted. It is the preliminary to any positive action.

Our world is changing more rapidly than ever before. We need dialogue to ensure that the changes are fruitful, to create agreement about the steps we should be taking. Discussion can lead to new and significant ideas which can be communicated. Can this cause change? Our answer depends on our view of human nature. An agreement to discuss assumes that human beings are motivated to discover their changing needs, that they are open to changing views of their needs, and that the future can be better than the past. We must not lose sight of this optimistic starting point. It is easy to conclude that change of the necessary magnitude is impossible and by so doing we insure failure through inaction.

We must first recognize how ill-prepared we are for the forms of discussion we need. We are used to authoritarian learning situations in which it was assumed that one member of the group knew and that the others should learn. Dialogue, however, assumes that we are looking for new patterns, many of which may not consciously be known to any member of the group. We must look for a creative meshing of ideas to create new patterns of action.

Let us be specific and consider the reasons for which people come together for dialogue, the few rules we know which help to create dialogue and the criteria for evaluation of a successful dialogue group.

People can be brought together in three kinds of frameworks: first, to perceive how they can personally act effectively in their world; second, to increase their understanding of the functioning of the world; and third, to decide what changes need to be made in the socioeconomic structures. The first type of group, devoted to individual growth, will be most likely to appeal to those who are not happy with their personal lives. The second type will appeal to those who feel that their opportunities for self development lie in greater understanding of the world. The third style of group will involve those who are dissatisfied with parts of the socioeconomic system, who want to understand it better in order to change it, and who feel that they have the action skills to effect such change. Each of these approaches is useful, and any fully successful group will involve all three elements. Each type of group and every experience of true learning must, however, recognize the constraints of the past, must hold a hope/belief for the future, and must act in the present.

Groups are created for many purposes. These rules apply to a group which is concerned both with the discovery of directions and with finding ways to achieve those directions.

Make sure that people get to know each other before the dialogue begins.

This rule is often reduced to "Be sure to make introductions," which destroys its purpose. Discussion of real issues requires trust; otherwise there will be surface chatter rather than meaningful dialogue. Each person present should spend at least one minute —

and preferably five — setting out the reasons why they are present, what they would like to achieve, what they think they can contribute, and where they would like the discussion to go. Each person should be aware of self-deprecating comments such as "I'm just . . . a housewife, an extra pair of hands, etc."

People will undoubtedly object that many discussions cannot be set up this way, for time is too precious. However, nothing significant will take place until people feel comfortable with each other, and this cannot be rushed. If you want to teach others about the future — and learn from them as well — you must take the time to get to know them.

Limit the size of your group.

There is an optimum size for dialogue groups: from eight to twelve. With less than eight people the range of experience is usually not sufficiently wide; with more than twelve the range of relevant experience is too great to handle easily. Experienced people can interact successfully with greater numbers.

Don't have a discussion leader.

This is difficult to implement, but it is still the best

single rule of thumb. A self-aware group does not need a discussion leader because the members of the group will know how to lead their own discussion. If the group is not yet self-aware, the task of a discussion leader is to eliminate her/his own leadership role as quickly as possible.

There are, of course, ways that the discussion leader can "steer" the group toward more rapid self-awareness, but the more s/he uses her/his authority, the slower the process will be. The group should chart its own course with the leader participating as an equal.

Deal fruitfully with individual differences.

The "group" should draw out the silent person, should become aware of her/his skills and ask for comments where relevant. The talkative individual, if s/he is really dominating the group, should be informed of her/his behavior by another member of the group who knows her/him — or eventually by a collective explosion. The group itself will learn to determine what the relevant point is and will control itself for its own purposes. The group should be particularly alert to inherent assumptions about the skills of particular classes of people. There is often a tendency to assume that white males between 35 and 65 have the most to contribute and to allow them to speak for as long as they wish while cutting off women, etc. The group as a whole should act to prevent this from happening. Each group is different; each situation requires a different style. Style must be based on the past and the future — the history of the individuals concerned and the hopes held for the future. The effort must be to find the immediate, feasible step which will move people the maximum distance from where they are to where they want to be.

Create a group myth.

A group starts to function effectively when it has created its own collective experience to which it can refer. This is likely to be humorous: a joke, a misunderstanding, a disaster turned into a success. This collective experience is often called a "myth," for it becomes a method of bringing the group together when it threatens to fall apart. It creates a group identity.

. . . Plus ten percent for risk.

In every case, too little risk is irrelevant and too much is dangerous. One rule of thumb is to find ways to permit people to do what they already can plus ten percent for risk. This rule can determine, for example, who should meet with whom. The meeting of someone with a relatively narrow, white "middle class" outlook with a black power advocate will probably be both irrelevant and dangerous. You should dialogue with someone whose world you can enter, and by entering it enlarge your own world.

How to measure the success of your group may be a bit tricky. Don't be afraid of "failure." In our statistical society, we like to measure the number of groups, the number of participants, the number of programs created. Unfortunately, these numbers are irrelevant when measuring effectiveness in terms of personal growth. Those who cannot learn in one group/situation should seek other routes and not become a negative force in a place which is personally unfulfilling. The group in turn should not see this as failure, but should realize that there are many styles of learning.

The psychic energy needed to create change can be generated by working with others with whom we can find bases for agreement, or it can be wasted in battles we cannot hope to settle and which may become meaningless as the future emerges. Dialogue assumes that the future can only be invented when we join together to celebrate our human potential and when we accord others the same right. We are all searching for ways to live creatively. Our different pasts ensure that we will find many different routes.

19 Community Involvement

This document is a dialogue focuser designed to help people perceive the issues of community participation. More and more communities across the country are involving citizens in thinking about their future. Which of these patterns are creative and which are counter-productive? Is community participation, with its promise of restoring democracy, what the Bicentennial should be all about?

One individual I know suggests that the development of community participation may be the least understood, and the most important, story of the mid-seventies.

Over the last hundred years communities have gradually lost control of their own directions and decision-making powers. Many people, confronted by complex systems of elected and bureaucratic officials, feel powerless to affect decisions. With the exception of the small number of people who vote, and the even smaller number of people who are active in community affairs, most people believe that "You can't fight city hall." Massive governmental bureaucracies have stepped into the void, creating giant systems that become more and more remote.

However, in the last ten years, there has begun a movement back to citizen participation. Today, the idea of community participation has become almost a "motherhood" issue. Everyone is in favor of participation and there are almost as many ideas about effective ways of encouraging participation as there are "experts" in the field. Communities must decide which ways are really effective in ensuring opportunities for people to participate in creating their future.

The Rationale for Citizen Involvement

This enthusiasm for citizen participation reveals a large-scale change in our attitudes. Until recently, we believed that our political structures were capable of making good decisions. Now, after Watergate and mini-Watergates in states and neighborhoods across the country, people are demanding that they be involved in making the decisions which determine the direction of their community.

As people have moved in this direction, a body of theory has evolved to rationalize what people have already decided. Many believe that it is impossible for one person to make a good decision for another, but that an individual can help or facilitate the decision-making process of another by providing him/her with relevant information. Similarly, many believe that a bureaucratic system cannot really understand what the citizens it is supposed to serve want for their future.

As a result, an ever-broadening range of techniques has been developed to permit people to state what they want. We have polls of all types: Some are technologically sophisticated, others are not. Dialogue skills make it easier for people to talk across cultural and class boundaries. Television can be used to clarify disagreements. However, behind all of the techniques lie some fundamental questions about the aims of citizen participation.

The Approaches to Citizen Participation

There are three basic approaches to citizen participation. First, there are those who propose citizen participation which provides better information to existing decision-making systems so they can be more responsive to citizen needs. This can be called the "citizen input" model. Second, many see great potential in modern technologies and believe that large-scale electronic citizen democracy has become feasible; this might be called an "electronic democracy" model. Third are those who say we need to create new, more responsive and responsible decision-making systems which permit those who are most active and informed to be involved in the decision-making process where they have skills and commitment. This can be called the "new leadership style" model.

1. Citizen Input

Some of the best-known existing citizen input activities are *Goals for Dallas, Alternatives for Washington,* and *Iowa 2000*. These programs have involved more people, more intensively, in thinking about their futures than any others.

In these and similar programs, citizens are provided with a carefully selected set of issues which they are asked to study. The purpose is to decide the priorities for the city or state for coming years and decades. Once the choices have been made by the citizen, existing private and governmental structures take on responsibility for ensuring the goals are met.

Supporters of this approach argue that it provides clear information about citizen concerns. They can point to changes in direction which are a direct result of these activities. These programs entail a minimum of waste and people can understand exactly what they are supposed to do.

Those who believe in the possibility of electronic democracy argue that this type of exercise is almost meaningless because it doesn't change existing decision-making patterns at all. They feel that what they describe as the overstructuring of the whole process (i.e. the alternatives presented for study are carefully selected by those in power) makes it impossible for the real concerns of the people to surface.

Those who are looking for a new type of leadership believe that nothing significant will happen until there is a change in the decision-making process. They want to find ways to involve more people with skills and drive in the actual decision-making process — people who are largely locked out by present electoral and bureaucratic procedures.

2. *Electronic Democracy*

For many people, the ideal democratic form was Athenian Democracy where everyone met together to make decisions as a group. There is now an extraordinary potential for computers to permit a variation on this all-embracing democracy. In effect, some people suggest that government be run by instant and continuing referenda. Citizens could and would voice their views on population, abortion, famine, and other such issues.

These advocates argue that if people could state their views on the urgent problems of the day, appropriate directions could be determined on the basis of referenda results. They assume that the people have a clearer sense of necessary directions than the leaders and they feel that leadership is unnecessary. While the technical problems are formidable, they are not impossible and the costs for a working system could be reasonable.

Those who believe in citizen input reject this model because they don't believe it is possible for people to make intelligent decisions; they believe that there has to be a leader to make sure that people move in the right direction.

Those who believe that the present decision-making process needs remodeling also reject this approach because, while they believe that people can make intelligent decisions about directions for their own lives, they also believe that the formidable tasks of moving us in new directions require special skill and competence. They feel some situations call for leadership, and that leadership continues to be necessary even though its style needs to be changed.

3. *New Leadership Styles*

Those who want to develop new leadership styles argue that the breakdown of our society comes from both the excessive concentration of decision-making power and the fact that authority is given to those who hold power positions rather than to those who have appropriate knowledge and competence. They see community involvement as opening up ways for competent people to become involved in decision-making.

This new leadership needs to be more flexible than current leadership. It needs to change and adapt as our situation does. In this view, a community is functional if it can find those who can work successfully on a problem or possibility as it emerges, spend as long as is required to come to some successful decision, and then be willing to disband. It means one works where one can, where one has competence and a willingness to commit oneself. A functioning community can organize itself rapidly and effectively to deal with disaster because it is not dependent on titles for organization, but rather it works with available skills.

From the point of view of the citizen input model,

this type of community involvement is messy: The process of trial and error required for people to find where they can take on responsibility seems unnecessary or even threatening. Critics do not understand the criterion for success, for community involvement activities seldom result in any major, coherent body of knowledge, and success is measured in terms of better interconnections in the community, more effective leadership, and more leadership potential.

Those who believe in electronic democracy do not see a significant change in the system with a new leadership style. They see the argument that the resulting leadership structure is open instead of closed as a cop-out.

Developing any citizen involvement model is going to require choices between models presented. Those willing to be involved will have to make the choices. We all know that the end result of any decision is not necessarily the one aimed for; in the sixties our efforts to create a more humane society often ended in less humanity. The directions in which our community involvement activities move will be one of the prime factors determining the future dynamics of our society.

20 North Dakota and the Bicentennial

The proposals for Bicentennial activity discussed in Part II of this book must be translated into specific action projects if anything worthwhile is to be achieved. The following interview between the staff of the Northwest Regional Foundation and Dan Selman, Director of the North Dakota State Bicentennial Office, shows what is going on in his state.

The style he is using is very different from that of the past. There are very few large-scale programs. There is, however, an attempt to restore a sense of potency to communities which have lost their direction and their sense of self-worth.

The Bicentennial is no panacea promising technological fixes for human breakdowns. It is a time when we can inspire communities and challenge them to create more human futures. We can no longer expect "victories" over our difficulties. Rather we must learn to celebrate continuing development toward humanity's full potential, to glory in the struggle, and to travel hopefully, realizing that we will never arrive.

FUTURES CONDITIONAL: I guess I would like to start out by asking you about the Bicentennial. Why are you excited about the Bicentennial?

DAN SELMAN: The way I understand the Bicentennial, and the way I am trying to make the Bicentennial go, is that in '76 the United States is going to be 200 years old. And that particular time can either be an opportunity for people to do some really constructive kinds of things for themselves, since they *are* the country, or it can just go by with a nod of the hat. And so to me it's an opportunity for people to have some fun — but basically to get together with each other, learn about each other, and get some cooperative efforts going. And that, at least to me, is part of what the American Revolution was trying to do — taking time to get constructive things going because people want to do them and because it means people controlling their own future and their own existence.

FC: Do you see people in North Dakota having the same idea of the Bicentennial as you do?

DAN: More and more. I was just reading through a series of clippings, and it's fun to hear people, in their own newspapers and letters to the editor, espousing the Bicentennial as a time for doing something constructive, rather than just doing some hoopla things. So they think their community should do something that will have some quality of life impact, that will have some lasting effect.

I think that North Dakota is probably fertile soil for this kind of thing, because people out here tend to be practical, and they get impatient with things that are just on the surface. If they're going to do something, they want to know why they should do it, and they want it to be something that is going to mean something to them. So they are particularly susceptible to the idea that the Bicentennial is a time for them to do something solid and constructive. I also think that it's much harder here, particularly in the small towns, to say that somebody else is responsible, because people know that if they don't do it, it's not going to happen. I believe I counted eleven cities in North Dakota with a population over 5,000, so that gives you a good feel of how rural the state is.

FC: What are people thinking about and doing for the Bicentennial?

DAN: Well, one thing that a lot of communities are doing is some type of community beautification, because it's an obvious thing. They're saying, "Let's clean up for the birthday party, let's create a better environment for the third century." This runs all the way from planting flowers to cleaning up riverfronts. One of our communities, Tioga, is face-lifting the business section and developing a Scandinavian motif.

FC: How do these things happen?

DAN: Somebody gets turned on by the idea. In virtually every community in North Dakota that I know of that's doing something, I could probably name one or two key people who got excited and said, "We're going to do it!" And they started pushing and other people caught the bug and it started happening.

FC: What do you do when somebody gets turned on in one of these towns? Do they come to you? Or are you somehow searching them out?

DAN: It's a combined thing. If we have any kind of basic strategy at all, it's been that I have spoken to as many state conferences of various types of groups as I can, and said, "You know, your community could do something really constructive for the Bicentennial. We have people who are willing to come out and help organize your community, to help your community think through what might be done and help your community set itself up to do something for the Bicentennial." Then of course we go in, we're invited in, and we try to reach as large a group of people as we can. And it just grows.

We do tell them that we, as a state commission, will not recognize their programs unless they have a committee that is broad-based and representative of the entire community. And we say, "To us, that means you have representatives of as many different organizations in your community as possible: that you have youth represented, that you have women represented, that the Chamber of Commerce and the Historical Society and the service clubs are involved." We say we just can't recognize their committee as being the official Bicentennial committee unless they have a lot of different people on it.

FC: Why would they want official recognition as a Bicentennial Community or committee?

DAN: First, everyone likes recognition, and that's basically what the Bicentennial Communities program is: recognition for a community that has a well-rounded Bicentennial program. We have also said that communities applying for funding of Bicentennial projects are probably going to have a better shot at it if they have a recognized Bicentennial committee. We also use the fact that, like all state commissions, we sell Bicentennial medallions and commemorative coins, and we sell them at a considerable discount to Bicentennial committees that are recognized by the state. These committees can then sell these medallions and coins to make money for their own programs.

I think we have tried to make constructive use of the national Bicentennial Community program. The communities get involved because they want the official recognition, they want to be one of the communities flying the official Bicentennial flag. Then we ensure that they organize fairly and responsibly by saying, "In order to qualify for recognition, you have to have a representative committee, you have to have a variety of kinds of projects in your community." So we encourage them to do a responsible job of planning and get a representative group involved in it.

FC: What are some of the small towns doing with the Bicentennial?

DAN: Well, some of them are doing things that people in the community have been thinking or talking about for quite awhile. I mentioned Tioga, the community that is redoing its entire business district. There have been people there who have been saying, "We really need to do this to spruce up our town" for eight or ten years. The Bicentennial has become the time to get it done. The town has a population of 1,500 and had been declining economically for years. But now they've created a lot of community spirit, and the town is functioning better today than it was a year ago. Part of it is that they used the Bicentennial, and the recognition that comes with being a Bicentennial Community, to pull the town together. They said, "See, this is a good program — the state of North Dakota recognizes it, the national program recognizes it," to get people in the community behind the project.

A lot of communities are doing Festival activities of course; they're having parades and picnics and pageants, those kinds of things. The major thing we push with communities doing these kinds of activities is for them to plan events that will include as many people in the community as possible. So if the school is going to do something, then they do something that will involve the rest of the community in the school. Or if the American Legion is planning an activity, they tie in with other community events, so that the events reinforce each other and get a lot of people involved, rather than being separate events of separate groups.

Here's a fun one — The city of Minot has, as one of their goals, a million red, white, and blue petunias by '76. Right now, kids are planting petunia seeds in their homes, in their classrooms, getting them started. Then they'll plant them outside when it gets warm enough. They really have some impressive splashes of red, white, and blue color on their hills, in front of business places, all over town. It also happens that our state horticulturalist thinks this is a fun idea, so he is experimenting with different types of petunias so that he can give communities specific suggestions as to what types will give the best definition of color. If they want to put the Bicentennial logo on a hill, he'll help them. Of course this doesn't have major significance for the future, but it's amazing how much involvement you can get with a project like that. Plus it's something that's highly visible, so the community can look and say, "Oh yeah, we're involved in that program."

As long as we're on flowers, some of the garden clubs in the state are tying their flower shows in with other community activities. This is what is happening in Hatten, North Dakota. Their Fourth of July celebration is going to have a horse show, an historical pageant, a flower show, and street dancing with a couple of different bands, so that the older people can have their music at one end of the block and the kids can have theirs at the other. It's just a matter of getting people to get together doing things they might otherwise be doing separately.

FC: What does a community of, say, 100 do?

DAN: Well, Knox, North Dakota, with a population of 115 or so, is making a monument to a school that no longer exists. They're also setting up a new park. The thing about communities that size is that people come from the whole area around to work together on these projects. Knox got a matching grant from the Bicentennial Commission for their marker, so they started having old-fashioned bake sales, ice cream socials, auctions, to raise a few dollars. Now I'm sure that not a month goes by but what they have some kind of Bicentennial event there. And they tell us that Knox has more life now than it's had in years. It's just the kind of community that all the sociologists have said will be gone in a few more years. Except that maybe now it won't be, because people are enjoying life together there now, and they're having social events that pull those people in the community together. Usually once the school is gone, the social center of the community dies. Right now the Bicentennial is becoming the social focus of some smaller towns. When we recognized Knox as an official Bicentennial community, 75 of the 115 residents showed up at the luncheon!

FC: What about the larger cities in North Dakota — what are they doing?

DAN: Well, Williston, which has a population of about 11,000, is putting together a pageant of American music — a chorus, a band, a barber shop quartet, Indian dancers — and taking it to Norway, where many of the residents are originally from, this summer. They have eight or ten concerts scheduled in Norway, and they'll say, "Hey folks, we're celebrating our Bicentennial. This is some of what America is musically. Why don't you come over and join us for the hoopla next summer when we do the 200th birthday?

FC: And this is a Bicentennial project? How are they raising the money?

DAN: The money for the tickets to Norway is their own responsibility. They are raising it through donations, by giving concerts in their own community, by serving as waiters and waitresses for anybody who holds a banquet meeting. Then they've received matching grants from the state commission to help cover some of the expenses for costumes, props, lighting, and so on.

FC: I've heard something about an oral history project in North Dakota. Is that tied in with the Bicentennial?

DAN: Yes, that's a state-wide project that was started with funds from the Bicentennial commission. The basic idea behind the oral history project is that in North Dakota we still have people living here who originally broke the sod, who went up and down the Missouri on steamboats, we have Indians who can remember their first sight of a white person. And so we have people going out and interviewing them. For example, we have about two hours of interview with an Indian woman who talks about building a sod house on the prairie at the turn of the century. The Bicentennial Commission put up the money for the first six months, and then we had the material evaluated so we could see what kind of material we were getting. The historians in the state really liked the material the interviewers were coming up with, so the Farmer's Union in North Dakota funded it for another year. Now we're trying to get the state legislature to pick up the funding for the final two years.

It's working out well, because a number of county historical societies are learning oral history interviewing techniques from our people and continuing the project in their area after our people have left. Then they're using some of the information in local historical booklets and that kind of Bicentennial project. The Bicentennial communities are also enthusiastic and are asking these people to come in to interview residents of the area, are providing names of potential interviewees. They have a schedule set up so that in three years they can cover the whole state. They've already got a fantastic collection of interviews.

FC: What about the future? Are towns using this Bicentennial as a time to think about the future?

DAN: It varies with the community. Some are basically using the Bicentennial as a city clean-up, improvement program, so they hope that in '76, '77, '78 they'll be able to keep their community spruced up. A number of areas are talking about senior citizen centers — getting those established in the community for the Bicentennial. Several communities are running community surveys through the newspapers, saying "What do you think we ought to do with the Bicentennial?" In Carrington, they want to have a park that specifically commemorates some of the Japanese people that lived in that community at one time and had a beautiful Japanese garden. And they are running community surveys asking, "Where do you think this park ought to go? Should it go in this spot in the community or over here by the highway?" This kind of questionnaire involves people in making some decisions.

Then we go all the way to the city of Fargo, which is very dramatically trying to involve its people in the future with a three day conference on the future (March 24-26, 1975) with Alvin Toffler and the architect Paolo Soleri, among others. We just met with the governor of North Dakota and he's agreed to keynote it. It is sponsored by the school system and the Bicentennial committee, and involves the entire school system in futures thinking. I've seen some of the material — they already have about forty courses lined up, with everything from "Women in the 21st Century" to "Genetic Engineering" to " Use of Computers" to "Religion in the 21st Century." And these programs will be available to everyone in the community.

This conference is being well publicized. But the people of Fargo are also involving public television in presenting a series of televised programs on alternatives for the future, projections of what the 21st century might be like — that kind of thing.

FC: Sometimes when I'm talking to people about the

Bicentennial, I get very apathetic responses like "Who cares?" Do you come across that very much in North Dakota?

DAN: Oh sure. But then I say, "Well, people in Tioga care; people in Minot care; people in Fargo care. And here is why they care — because they're able to do these kinds of things in their community." Gee, they never thought of the Bicentennial that way. And I think this is part of our success in North Dakota. We've kept a fairly low profile with the Bicentennial and didn't try to get a lot of publicity until we were in a position to point specifically to a community and say, "Look. They're doing this as their way of celebrating it." And of course I have community leaders who say, "Ah, you're putting me on. There is no way Bottineau can do that kind of program," and I tell them, "Well, I'm sorry, but the people in Bottineau don't know that and they're doing it." So, once you have communities that are actually doing something, other people start to believe that you can do it.

FC: Do you feel that this Bicentennial activity is going to make communities different after the Bicentennial? Or do you see it as more or less a one-shot thing?

DAN: Well, my hope and goal, and I think we're getting at it somewhat, is that, because of the kind of activity that people are doing for the Bicentennial — just the fact that garden club people, the American Legion and the local high school are sitting down and talking about the same project — lines of communication that haven't been open for awhile are going to be opened. We believe that just the process of the community having to work together in deciding what they ought to do for the Bicentennial, the process of struggling with the decisions, is going to make people start wanting a piece of the action in making decisions on how other things go in their communities. I know that some lines of communication that weren't there before are opening up in communities now. I think of a community like Tioga, with the things they are doing for the Bicentennial. They managed to have a community-wide, ecumenical church service for the first time in ten or twelve years. Not necessarily because they have new religious leaders in there, but because they had people in their community working together on Bicentennial projects, and they had a community celebration for the whole weekend. And they said, "We have to have our community worshipping together, too." Some of the lay people just flat out said to the pastors who were hanging up on the theological rationale, "We're going to do it!" I think just the fact that people are starting to insist that "We are going to start to function as a community and be bigger than some of our differences," because they worked for the Bicentennial together is a healthy step.

FC: What do you see happening in 1976?

DAN: Well, hopefully, the few people who have gotten involved in working with other people in the community will stay hanging in there because they start to see that as people do things together the community works better. In North Dakota I really see people just plainly becoming more responsible citizens on the local level.

I do have some vague hopes that maybe the Bicentennial will serve as a spur to get some future-oriented thinking going statewide. Right now, it's far too premature to start talking about that. There are some people who are getting turned on to future thinking, future planning.

I'm also one of the great sceptics of the Bicentennial, along with my enthusiasm for it. The Bicentennial is not going to be the salvation of many communities or of the United States. We're going to have a troubled time in this country. There are going to be many who will raise serious questions about the survival of the U.S. during the Bicentennial times. There are economic questions being raised right now. I do think that, along with that, there are ways of giving people constructive alternatives for what they can do during this rather frustrating time. And so I'm trying to point people to the constructive alternatives and what they can do if they'll cooperate locally. Hopefully this cooperative experience will keep going at a local level — gradually percolating up beyond that — and some people will learn that they have the capability of changing things when they get involved.

In the months since this interview, a nationwide movement has started to develop proposing that Bicentennial activities continue through 1991, the anniversary of the adoption of the Bill of Rights. The rationale behind this idea is that it took fifteen years to create the United States: It may well take as long to recreate the country.

PART IV: Questions, Questions, Questions

The following questions emerged from my visit to Maryville College in Maryville, Tennessee. A group of students; a professor, and I decided that we wanted more out of my visit than just another speech. We therefore set up a process which would generate questions which I would answer, without previously knowing them, during the period in which I would normally have lectured.

There were several sets of questions asked by different groups; they are divided from each other here so that you can perceive the varied directions in which individuals/groups, confronted by an open-ended opportunity, may move. On page 234, the questions which were chosen as most challenging are listed. Do you agree with the selection or would you have chosen differently?

I've included these questions here in the belief that they may spark your interest in new areas of thinking. They may also help you decide the directions in which you want to explore further.

21 Questions, Questions, Questions

What is truth?

Why can't we answer these questions?

Why can't a man live in the presence of his future?

Who controls socialized medicine and socialized mental health care?

How do you get this country to lay down all of its nuclear weapons?

Why do we need to ask questions?

How do you see the future of the United States in terms of government and people? Will she continue to be a viable force or will she decay and crumble?

How do you see the role of homo sapiens? Will we continue in our present role or will we be surpassed by another form of life?

Is the Maryville ideal (small liberal arts of education) a viable one for the future?

What form will secondary education take in the future?

What is the future of the military-industrial complex?

What sort of dominating political and national systems does the future hold?

What sort of housing and housing systems does the future hold?

How can we make (and keep) people aware of their surroundings?

What sort of future does the Constitution have?

How can we develop the human community?

What can *one person* do to make the future more pleasant for the rest of humanity?

Will there be a World War III?
If so, when and how?

Are the fine arts dying?

What sort of questions are asked consistently across the nation?

What shape is your "book" in?
What is the purpose of this "book" and the travels?

What are you doing anyway?

How big a part in our future will God play?

What is the future of religion?

What does the future hold in terms of physical and mental health?

How long till solar energy is put into use in the U.S.?

Will there be any increase in outer space research? Why?

Will cloning be developed into an acceptable and viable procedure?

What is your opinion on the recent abortion-manslaughter charge?

Does Theobald think that the United States will have to revert to socialism to solve our economic problems?

What is the possibility of the underdeveloped countries raising their standard of living?

Will the private schools survive the economic crisis?

Do you think the United States should become more simplistic in its standard of living and, if yes, how would Theobald go about accomplishing this?

How could the public school systems be changed to meet the needs of the society?

Do you think the environment will be sacrificed (for instance, strip-mining, off-shore drilling)?

What can be done to help the elderly become more of an active part of our community?

How do we increase employment but not increase the production of unnecessary goods?

Do you think the countries of the world will be coerced to become world-conscious?

Are suffering and pain a necessity for compassion and growth?

What's the future of football and other spectator sports?

Should man be more oriented toward "self-law" or the laws which society has laid down for him to follow?

Is it necessary to have a higher education to cope with problems of today's society?

According to the recent question of abortion as seen in Boston, at what point does life begin (e.g., at birth, fertilization, etc.)?

Do you feel that present day methods of agriculture and even new experimental methods will be able to feed the spiraling population of the future?

Should the man of the future look to space for his resources, or should he look towards science to invent new methods to make us independent of raw materials?

Human cruelty — why?
There must be an end . . . to it.
A way to a nobler way of life.
Values of power and knowledge of technique
Are empty; values of compassion and that sort
of human values lead . . . into a mist-shrouded
valley . . . that is . . . to uncertain futures . . .
What . . .
Are we alone? Is there something out there in that
other world . . . in the mist?

What will the arms buildup lead to?

When will a Negro become President?

When will the East Coast become entirely urban?

Will a democratic government hold up in the U.S.A.?

What will follow a democratic government in America?

When is the time of no-return technologically?

Does the U.S. give a damn about the rest of the world?

Does anybody give a damn?

What direction will morals take? Liberal?
Conservative?

How far will education go?
What does it get you?

How can we continue to allow some people to be manipulated while others are advancing?

Will there ever be equality among all?

Can we continue economically in this profiteering society?

Does anybody give a damn about anybody else?
Anything?

What direction will (a) education (b) morals
(c) economy go?

How can we continue to allow some people to be manipulated while others are advancing?

A lot of young people, it seems to me, are very lonely — they can't relate to any activity, endeavor, or other constructive development—and to most other people.

Is this a disadvantage and weak point in the new life style philosophy — "do your own thing" or "anti-organization — don't organize — let things happen"?

I feel this has led to many, many lonely young people — bored young people — who turn to drugs to relieve their boredom.

I think this campus could be an exciting place on which to be—on weekends—and other special times — if student leaders were willing to organize groups or focal points in which campus-wide activities could be created — activities need group work and support in order to succeed — consistently (50% of the time?)

What's wrong with "the striving for excellence," trying to be *the best* at something? Isn't the new life style (Con III) saying — mediocrity is enough — it's too hard (and inconvenient) to try to strive toward excellence?

How does one find entry points to change the system?

Who the hell cares?

Is the system worth getting into?

What's a system?

Are we right in trying to change?

Do we really have power to change things?

Why do we want to change?

Why doesn't everybody elect me officer-king?

Why do we find it so difficult to ask questions?

Are nuclear energy people brainwashed?

Why can't faculty at Maryville College have raises?

How much fact is in the news we receive?

Robert Theobald, do you care? Or are you just after money? Why do you do what you do? Why should I care? I won't even be here in three months.

Can Maryville College ever make a difference in society?
What society?

Why is it that I don't see any questions in "flashing lights?"

What is relevant enough to make a difference?

Was Richard Nixon a crazy man? Or are we all crazy? Are we all Bo-Zo's on this bus?

Does American government really care about people?

Why is there suffering?

Where is the fine line between persuading people that you're right, and twisting their arm?

Is truth just persuasion?

Are you listening?

Education

(a) What should education prepare us for?

(b) Will the educational system, as a system, last? should it last?

(c) Is there a need for redefining the purpose of education, especially at the college level, i.e., are we learning what we should be learning in order to be fulfilled and an integral part of society?

Ethics

(a) How can we solve the ethical conflicts that arise in such situations as marriage, family, sexuality, etc.?

(b) How can we practice what we preach, put theory into practice?

Awareness

(a) How can we stop the exploitation of others politically, economically, materially, etc.? Is international unification the answer?

How do we create livable surroundings for large groups of people, in terms of architectural considerations?

Loneliness of the young — disadvantage or advantage? How do we increase personal and social interactions on a college campus?

Is excellence a worthwhile goal?

Can culture support multiple lifestyles? How do you do experiments in lifestyle?

How do adults respond to values of the young?

How do people of diverse values work together?

How do you establish and do you want to establish consistency in ethical practices on Sunday and on a weekday?

Do environmental conditions affect values?

Can there be value systems applicable of broader conditions?

Can we afford to set aside questions of values and adult/young conflicts while finding solutions to food/space/population questions?

What is quality education?

How does a grading system affect the search for education? Can we do away with grades?

What are the goals of students? If they have none, why not? How do we lead them to goals they will find worthwhile?

Are goals necessary?

In what direction is religion going? Is the role of the church becoming less important or will it become more important?

Are our natural resources truly running out? What about those vast untouched lands?

Will there ever be a "war to end all wars?" If so, will it put an end to us all?

Will man ever create other human life (test tube babies)?

Will society ever pull out of its present apathetic slump?

Due to the still rapidly growing world population, is there a possibility that man could build underwater cities as a new habitat? if so, how soon could we expect to live in the ocean?

What will the government do to solve the ecological problems of the world when it is so involved in capitalism and exploitation of resources?

Please explain what a "futurist" is, and what role he plays in the determination of *our* future.

With the various crises and shortages in the United States today, what type of future do you see for the small private or independent liberal arts colleges such as Maryville?

These are the questions actually asked:

How do people of diverse values work together?

Please explain what a "futurist" is, and what role he/she plays in the determination of *our* future.

Who the hell cares?

Is it necessary to have a higher education to cope with problems of today's society?

What's the future of football and other spectator sports?

Do you think the environment will be sacrificed to solve our economic problems (for instance, strip-mining, off-shore drilling)?

How do you see the future of the United States in terms of government and people? Will she continue to be a viable force or will she decay and crumble?

What can *one person* do to make the future more pleasant for the rest of humanity?

PART V: Futures Conditional

Previous editions of this book have listed *Opportunities for Involvement*. The pace of change in society is now so great that it is unrealistic to pretend that a book which will hopefully stay in print for several years can provide a viable summary of available possibilities because the most exciting initiatives are often the most fragile.

Let me therefore list two steps which you can take. First, if you believe that you're interested in being involved, drop us a line stating that you've read *An Alternative Future for America's Third Century* and that you'd like to learn what is being done to create a more human future. We'll send you a mailing which will give you information about our efforts and ways that you can get involved.

If you're committed to these ideas already, we hope that you'll subscribe to *Futures Conditional*, our continuing periodical which will bring you information ten times a year about the process of *creating* America's Third Century. The price is $20.00. We're aware that this is high, but we have no foundation support for the publication. If you can't afford the dollars, we suggest you convince your public library, your school or college library, or a relevant group in your town that they should be involved.

The theme of *Futures Conditional* is that change is not only necessary but possible. However, it can only be created if more of us commit ourselves to helping people see the necessity for change and providing contexts for creating new directions. Now that you've completed this book, my colleagues and I hope you'll join with us to create desirable directions.

PART VI: Feedback

These responses followed the distribution of a pre-publication edition of this book. Names and addresses are given so that other readers may correspond. However, please limit yourself to the mail until you have established contact and determined your mutual interests.

Many of the issues raised by these letters are discussed in *Teg's 1994: An Anticipation of the Near Future* (1970) by Robert Theobald and J. M. Scott. The book is a futuristic novel which takes a backward look at the remainder of the century via a series of dialogues. The initiator of these dialogues is Teg, a young woman recipient of a George Orwell Fellowship which was established ten years previously in celebration of the fact that 1984 was not as bad as it might have been. Interested readers may obtain *Teg's 1994* from The Swallow Press, Chicago.

RESPONSE 1

I just finished reading "An Alternative Future for America's Third Century." It is outstanding material.

My comment is directed not towards what is in the book, but towards what I sense the book still needs.

You cover the whole range of issues — from new modes of thought to new global relationships. It is a conceptual tour de force.

What is needed, so it seems to me, is that element which reaches inside the spirit of the reader and touches his emotion as well as his intellect. You have given lavishly of your mind. It needs now the deeper dimension that can only come from some delicate expression of your heart and soul.

Please don't take offense at this. But I am inclined to think people must be drawn by a hope and a promise as well as be driven by a danger and a fear. For what is involved, in my view, is not simply a mechanical shift in thought, but the growth of a deeper insight and an expanded awareness. That is an organic process which takes place, in part, within the spirit of a person and a society.

What I am talking about is intangible, and each man can only express it in his own way. I know from what I have read of your other material that you have a depth of spirit and a range of personal conviction that can provide that dimension which is currently lacking in most public discussion on these issues. I believe if you could add that element to the considerable presentation you have already made, you would have a combination which would both grip people with the reality of our circumstances, and inspire them to reach forward with an enthusiasm which, while out of style, is essential to any significant step forward in our affairs.

W. V. Wishard
1805 Wainwright Drive,
Reston, VA 22090

RESPONSE 2

I was happy to see the *FC* pre-publication edition of the newest *Alternative Future*. Besides enjoying it for itself — as a well-put-together and, I think, useful piece of work — I've been grateful for the occasion it's given me to look back to '76 Week, now almost a year in the past. *(This was an effort to bring together people to discuss the issues in this book. R. T.)*

I was awfully depressed when I got back from Spokane last November. From a personal perspective, I felt I hadn't met whatever expectations you had had in bringing me there. But in a larger perspective, too, I sensed that many people's expectations for each other, for the event, and for themselves hadn't been fulfilled. I sensed that you — and many of the rest of us — had somehow hoped for a whole new spirit to coalesce in Spokane, and go forth from there to bring on the Great Transformation. That clearly didn't happen.

Or did it? What strikes me now is that if paradigms are invisible to those who hold them ("Whoever it was that discovered water, we can be sure it wasn't a fish"), then paradigm-shift, too, must be invisible to the people participating in it. If you're in a universe which doubles in size every second, you will never know that fact. By analogy, if fundamental change *is* happening in our culture, those of us involved in it will be the last to recognize it. In the meantime, we become frustrated waiting for something that we can touch or see.

What I like best about *An Alternative Future for America's Third Century* is that it gives us some hopeful things to see and touch, at the same time, of course, reminding us that more are needed. I haven't gone back for another look at the first two versions, so this comparison may not be accurate, but this book seems more grounded in the seeable and touchable. If that's the case, it may prevent some of the frustration — the sense of expectations unfulfilled — that I felt on returning from Spokane.

(I'm glad that my "future autobiography" technique could serve as one of those seeable, touchable things — although I don't think you gave yourself enough credit for its first use in *Teg*.)

In retrospect, I suspect that '76 Week was successful — in making subtle but significant changes in quite a few people. In my own case, at least, I can trace specifically to Spokane some differences in the rest of my graduate work last spring and some changes in the way I'm working and living now. Have any others said similar things?

A final change of subject: have you written down anywhere your talk on the requirements of all systems to operate — and the way those requirements are identical to the traditional virtues of love, honesty, etc.? I've been using the point in discussions, but would like to see it in expanded form — and to know its originator, if other than you.

Thanks again for the book. Keep on with your good works; let me know anything I can do to help.

Kenneth W. Davis
Apartment 114
2150 Richmond Road
Lexington, KY 40502

RESPONSE 3

I was much tempted to write a scenario as you suggested. I have a scenario in mind, but my writing of it would no doubt benefit me more than you. In view of your limited time, I will direct my thoughts to the book.

I would guess that it has two phases, negative and positive. The negative phase is to persuade your audience that what they take for reality (their present life-style) is in fact an illusion; the positive phase is to engage them in the process of developing a sounder illusion. (More durable, reliable, less damaging, more humane, more viable in every respect . . . not a bigger pie, or a smaller pie, but a different pie.)

If this analysis has some validity, it prompts the formulation of some questions:

What are the ingredients that make an illusion accepted as real?

What methods may legitimately and effectively be used for illuminating the illusory character of what others now accept as real? (You do a lot of this; have you codified your methods?)

What ingredients should an illusion have to warrant acceptance as real? (That is, as a workable illusion, an illusion that can muster enough supporting evidence to make it credible and workable.)

You are in the process of myth building; have you codified the required ingredients?

What illusion is available or constructible that will meet these standards?

To what extent must people accept an illusion as real in order for it to be workable?

Is this changing? Can some people now commit themselves to a tentative illusion (or definition of reality) . . . . ("Commit themselves" means act upon.)

How conscious can people be of the limits of an illusion and have it still retain or gain their acceptance in practice?

We now have many definitions of reality, or mythologies, or symbolic systems, or paradigms, or even scenarios, each of which has *totalitarian pretensions*. Each is, in its own way, an illusion, but strong in its hold on populations or decision-makers (seems real enough to them) because its validity is supported both by common agreement, by perceived supporting events, and by lack of perception of contrary events. Totalitarianism maintains its reality by narrowing the range of perceived events (censorship) and by creating perception or visibility for its realities (propaganda). By this analysis, military hardware is propaganda; its existence makes real the threat of a designated enemy. The threat of the exhaustion of earth's resources and the threat of bringing on its own head the destruction of both sides are lesser realities.

If we are not temporarily interrupted by a new narrow gauge political, economic, or military totalitarianism, we may be able to move into an new era in which each definition of reality will command allegiance only in the context of an accepted group of viabilities and in the presence of recognized and accepted limits and risks.

Human nature being what it is, there must be some securities. My intuition is that these securities will be found not in buttressing present shaky illusions but in the quality of communications in communities and among communities. Is this not hinted at in *Teg's 1994*?

I find that I tend to agree with the process in which you are engaged more than with the content. You are engaged in illuminating the illusory aspects of people's realities; you are engaged in an effort to enlist people in the development of more adequate paradigms and myths. Are you implying the possibility of a new and better totalitarian definition of reality, or a new and better tentative definition of reality? I repeat my two major questions from above: have you codified your negative and positive methods, and have you codified your criteria for adequate myths?

I do not know anything about the people who are part of your team, except for an exchange of letters with Nancy. What is the basis of your own cohesion? How much of it is agreement about content, and how much of it is engagement in process? How much of your cohesion is based on undiscovered illusions you may have about each other's realities? How much of the total communication among your key people is on high risk levels?

This set of questions is essentially on the same point as I raised at the first of this letter. Each definition of reality is inadequate and therefore vulnerable to revelations of its limitations and illusory character. Our predicament is particularly prickly right now because revelations of inadequacy are popping up in many areas at once. The economic system, for example, is vulnerable to analysis which lengthens the time cycle of the cost-benefit formula application, or broadens the base to acknowledge the contribution to "profit" made by exploited peoples. Those who borrow heavily from their fellow passengers must face a day of reckoning some day; when people perceive that the date of that day of reckoning may fall within their own lifetime, their illusion becomes visibly more precarious. At that point, it is much more likely to be vigorously defended than abandoned (see Rhodesia).

At the other end of the spectrum, each of us has a self-image which is supported by the response we get from our social context and by whatever level of satisfaction we achieve for our own deepest needs and drives. Our personal definition of who we are as individuals, whether articulated or not, is precarious in new ways. Social contexts are much more transitory than they used to be; those who today perceive their own fulfillment in their association with us may change overnight, as may we. Such fragile social contexts may not prove to be the most hospitable climate for communication at high risk levels. Yet *high risk communication is essential,* in my view, *for improving the quality of perceived reality.* Looking inward, every situation in which we find ourselves and every personal commitment satisfies some of our inner needs while holding others at bay. Fortunate indeed is he who can engage in high risk communication with himself without being immobilized or falling victim to his own chaos.

Therefore I add a third question to the ones about method and criteria: what do you recognize, Bob, as the core of your own strength?

I sometimes call our age "the age of revelation"; this, for me, is the same as calling it "the age of disillusionment." The tools of perception have been improved beyond our powers to anticipate. Time lapse photography and its analogues in the study of social history, the electron microscope and its analogues in statistical psychology, nuclear physics and transactional analysis, computer models and organizational dynamics, radiation and extrasensory perception, D.N.A. and information & communication technology, to name a few sources, are pouring new evidence on us. Try as we may to enlist each new revelation in the service of existing definitions of reality, the new evidence always, sooner or later, illuminates the inadequacy of our current definitions and brings to birth new realities we are forced to define.

When the context of analysis is insulated from the social fabric and from our own personality structures, so that the redefinition can take place in relative detachment, as in the present revisions in physics (e.g., quarks), the process can engage many brilliant minds and proceed with steady pace. But when the context of analysis is interlocked with the social structure and with the value systems that support our own personalities, the added complications are unsettling, to say the least. We proceed under many perils: disturbance of treasured relationships, loss of support by the very people who are needed for continuance, falterings in our own morale, clouding and shifting of accustomed reference points for navigation, multiplication of options without relevant criteria for limiting them to achieve a realistic focus for commitment and action. This leads to a fourth question: what is your game plan for handling the revelation and disillusion overloaod? If you don't have one, don't be surprised if everyone you talk to turns into a Rhodesian.

I recognize, Bob, that you operate under a great sense of urgency and have a well-articulated sense of direction; your objective appears to be to achieve acceptance of a new paradigm based on communications and a new myth based on broad participation and diversity. Where I am astray in my interpretation of your program, please correct me; your efforts to answer the four key questions I raise above will be very welcome indeed.

J. H. Vowles
106 Donlea Drive
Toronto, Canada M4G 2M5

RESPONSE 4

This is written in response to the pre-publication issue of Futures Conditional Vol. III No. 5 article, "Entering the Eighties: A Time for Despair."

I suggest that another "80s" scenario might emerge if a whole new attitude were generated. I am insufficiently familiar with all affecting factors to generate a detailed picture, but the skeleton might include the following tenets.

I Everyone must eat, be clothed and housed at a respectable comfortable level.

II Automation and technical improvements enable us to dispense with most arduous work outside of service industries and management of people.

III The anomie society encourages the need for people to find a listening, empathic ear.

Solutions

I Heavy research emphasis on continued development of automation techniques in building, transportation, cleaning, manufacturing, communication, health diagnosis, and treatment.

II Establishment of two kinds of centers:

A. Free mercantile and food centers where people go and obtain whatever they need.

Check out will be simply a listing of items obtained and recording in computer by name, address, and social security number.

A monthly record (statement) will be sent.

B. Job Centers:

1. Temporary centers where person goes each day he/she wishes to indicate availability, picks job, and goes. Employers call in needs, employee's arrival, time worked, satisfaction, and all is computer-recorded on record of employer and employee. No money exchange. Computer assigns value which is correlated with above (usage) and sent to each as part of monthly statement.

2. Contract centers where person indicates skills and contracts to work hours, days for specified number of weeks, months, or years.

   Computer recording as in II B.1. above.

   All credit in excess of usage (IIA above) may be used for travel, larger apartment (in excess of one bedroom per two adults, all living quarters would include bath, living room, dining room, kitchen), contract for private house, private car, employment of help, etc.

III All basic services:

Heat, light, energy sources, transportation would be government controlled.

Since everyone would have basic necessities, crimes against property should practically disappear.

Prestige would come from working and work position, not material acquisition.

International

I Every country would introduce a birth control plan to maintain the population at or below current level.

II An exchange value placed on every resource, whether food, energy, manufacturing, or expertise. Said items to be shared on a value-for-value exchange.

III Free movement of people among countries (assuming credits exceed debits thus permitting the travel of said persons). Countries may require specified amounts of excess credits for emigration.

IV Removal of import-export duties since value and need is established internationally.

Advantages

Nothing worth stealing since everything is free.

Barriers to movement removed and decisions to work or move based on personal achievement need.

Prestige based on production and self-behavior rather than external social pressures, hunger, or cold.

I hope this generates some additional thinking around the Institute and perhaps some strategies for implementation. I agree that current directions of humans sound like The Rise and Fall . . . . I don't think the fall is necessary. We are smarter than lemmings, I hope. I would like to hear your reactions to the ideas and do hope they are not duplicates of ones you have considered and discarded.

Mary T. Howard, Ph.D.
Dean of Student Services
Hestes Community College
475 Grand Concourse
Bronx, N.Y. 10451

RESPONSE 5

I am intrigued by your "looking backwards" technique of futures scenarios, in despair and in hope. Indeed, the Italian government is floundering today. With my experience currently, despair is an easy soft spot in the ice to fall through. And where are the powerful ready to share their power, or the deschamisados ready to cooperate to create their power? I like your emphasis that "power tends to distort information," but the powerful often want the distortion.

You say, "This task" (of understanding "creatively the new institutions") "can only be achieved if we provide citizens with meaningful information and opportunities for involvement." I am surprised that you haven't said more explicit things about the volunteerism movement. Indeed, in my capacity as Co-chairperson of the Information Committee of the Association of Voluntary Action Scholars, may I invite you to join that association and that committee (just forming)?

Your "Indeed, it may well be that our present perceptions of who are the 'good guys' and the 'bad guys' form one of the major blocks against creating effective action coalitions. It is not necessarily those who talk loudest or most liberally about the present situation who are most willing to act," strikes home. I have this open view toward communication, yet none the less have "failed" in getting this communication going. You say, "The second Copernican Revolution will only be possible if very many of us act together in the search for the communications era paradigm and the types of societies which it will create." Amen. But who is listening?

I am particularly interested in your "leaders as servants" versus "leaders on white horses." My own phrasing of this, recognizing that leaders have leaders and are themselves only part of the power structure is to contrast "loyalty up" the power structure versus "loyalty down." Do your efforts lead to the accumulation of power — accepted by those in power if the accumulation accrues to them — or to the distribution of power? My orientation is to the distribution of power — so I seem to end up tangling with bosses . . .

You say, "People . . . need to be able to find out what is going on in their local areas, the activities which need to be carried out and the opportunities for them to be involved. Second, they need to understand the massive forces which are presently changing the shape of the world and producing new problems and possibilities." It is for such an individual search through the massive thicket of detail that I have developed the "interactive book" methodology, and we have produced Information Resources for Public Interest. The local detail is not yet there, but the method is there to add it, yet not obscure others' searches for their own detail.

So here I sit, responding to your relaying of Ken Davis' suggestion of attempting to write my autobiography for the next twenty years. Wow. But for the nonce, I feel rather vincible. Shattered ego strength. Coerced. "In the future we must end the use of coercive power and authority; the ability to demand action on the basis of one's hierarchical position." Your suggestion of a guaranteed income as a way to cut economic authority is of great interest, but the accumulators of income don't seem about to accept that distributive procedure. But I do "celebrate," "live in the future," and even write poetry . . . Or I used to write poetry—haven't recently.

Carl C. Clark

RESPONSE 6

"Entering the Eighties: A Time for Despair":

> This negative scenario does not allow for technological solutions to problems — food from the

sea and use of solar energy. The problems of cities, which may be true for U.S. cities, are not necessarily the same as urban problems in other parts of the world. These problems need looking at for possible solutions to U.S. difficulties.

"Impact of the Seventies: Reasons for Hope":

Although the paragraphs on life-long learning are already becoming part of our educational system, I believe that there are very few reasons for hope given. How these positives did or could come about is not mentioned. No discussion of economics or resources is included. "Religion as a driving force" seems most unlikely to me as described here. Although I do believe there are reasons for hope, I did not find them in this scenario.

"Communication Realities and the Conservative Revolution":

I thought this one of the finest pieces in the book — certainly applicable to the U.S. and western European countries.

"Environmental Agreements":

Among whom were the agreements made? Without this information the chapter had little value to me.

"The Second Copernican Revolution":

Really enjoyed this chapter. The portions "What is the New Paradigm?," "The Dilemma of Education," and "The Reasons for Hope" MUST be communicated to all persons in decision-making positions by those aware of that need

OR

those aware of the needs for the new era must get *themselves* in the decision-making positions!

"Income Distribution and Social Change":

What are the possible economic arrangements to provide for a guaranteed annual income? What sort of educational effort is necessary for Americans to accept the idea of a few people working hard enough at lowered income, to provide an income for an increased number of persons?

Specifically, what will those persons receiving a guaranteed income do for the rest of society which will make them acceptable to the providers?

"The Potential of the Bicentennial":

The problems of and in the United States are not necessarily those of most of the rest of the world. WE are not going to make the determinations for those people unless through some influence in the United Nations — or some other worldwide structure.

"Past, Present and Future":

I agree that the best and most successfully workable long range alterations in beliefs should be made by information which is credible. Unfortunately reality is often otherwise and MUST be dealt with. Peoples' beliefs ARE coerced every day, in subtle and effective fashion, for example by churches, by employers, by husbands, and by any persons or groups with power to influence with information which may or may not be credible.

"How to Dialogue":

One of the most practical and useful chapters — very constructive. It would appear that groups or individuals with widely divergent viewpoints, however, probably cannot dialogue directly. It will be necessary then to have a successive meeting of groups which already interface — a long, hard, realistic approach.

"North Dakota and the Bicentennial":

In so far as the Bicentennial can help people of a given community or state to focus on long range solutions to problems, and general betterment of the region, and to generally improve their understanding of the many facets of state or regional problems and possible solutions, it can be very beneficial. In so far as it is used to promote unrealistic returns to "the good old days," I see it as potentially harmful to the community. Citizens must watch carefully to prevent negative attitudes from developing out of Bicentennial programs.

Karline M. Tierney
AAUW 21st Century Topic Chairman

1025 E. Lakeview Drive
Baton Rouge, LA 70810

(In an accompanying letter, Karline Tierney stated: "It interested me that although I did the writing and the comments in October, I only now got round to writing it out to you and found that I no longer agree with some of the things I had written in October.)

RESPONSE 7

I received your *Alternative Future for America's Third Century* a short time ago. What follows are some rather random comments in regard to sections of the book.

When I read the chapter on "Communication Realities and the Conservative Revolution," I was reminded of a book which I read in 1968. The title of that book is *Reclaiming the American Dream,* and its author is Richard Cornuelle. The thesis of the book is that it is a gross misreading of American history to see it as a constant struggle between the "public sector" and the "private sector." For between them there lies a vast "independent sector" of potential social action.

The starting point of Cornuelle's thought is a passage from de Tocqueville's *Democracy in America* (Volume

II, Second Book, Chapter V in the Vintage edition):

> The Americans make associations to give entertainments, to found seminaries, to build inns, to construct churches, to diffuse books. . . .
>
> Only those associations . . . in civil life without reference to political objects are here referred to. The political associations that exist in the United States are only a single feature in the midst of an immense assemblage of associations in that country.
>
> The political and industrial associations strike us forcibly; but the others elude our observation because we have never seen anything of the kind . . . they are as necessary . . . as the former and perhaps more so . . . the progress of the rest depends on the progress it has made.

Cornuelle's book is a Vintage paperback. I commend it to you.

I found your chapter on the impact of violence stimulating. Is it violence or *violation* which characterizes so much of modern life?

Your essay on the Second Copernican Revolution and Social Change reminds me of an anecdote (delightful because it is apocryphal) about Eli Whitney. The problem confronting him when he visited his friends the Greene family was how to reduce the overhead involved in producing cotton. It soon appeared that the stumbling block was the arduous labor it required to separate the seeds from the cotton. His failure to find a means of pulling the seeds out of the cotton caused him frustration. He then indulged in what I call "creative cheating." He simply changed the terms of the problem and sought a way to pull the cotton out of the seeds. The result was a week-end project. The rest, as they say, is history.

You give a printout based on a hypothetical NEA task force. Is this your way of stating that the NEA can be change-agent in a creative sense? Related to this is the question regarding who in the NEA seems to offer a potential role as a change-agent. And finally, if such persons are there, have you established any meaningful liasion with them?*

I share your concern with education. Some of these dilemmas have been resolved in my mind by remembering that there are really four disciplines — obser-

---

* *Author's Note:* The positive scenario in this volume is attributed to the American Association of Community and Junior Colleges as I have found it more open than the NEA to these questions.

vation, perception, analysis, and synthesis. The aim of education is to work with those disciplines; what we call subject-matter areas are simply vehicles for them. Humanities courses or interdisciplinary experiences are visible expressions of this. Mini-courses, such as those suggested by Charles Keller, former director of the John Hay Fellows program for high school humanities teachers, are another way of carrying through on this.

One such mini-course might be a study of the U.S. Constitution together with William Golding's *Lord of the Flies*. Another might deal with Alexis de Tocqueville and Charles Darwin, two young men who took ocean voyages in 1831. There are many other possibilities.

You mention from time to time synergy and certain qualities such as honesty, love, and respect for others. Perhaps an application of this might be recording "A" grades for all students at the beginning of a major unit or phase of study and having those grades stand unless and until the students show that they do not deserve them. Creative cheating? Maybe — or maybe not. (I'm planning to do it this year, for the first time.)

Finally, I'm enclosing something my wife gave me at a time when it seemed (and indeed was) badly needed. Perhaps it will be of use to you in your work. The text goes as follows:

> Every man has to seek in his own way to make his own self more noble and to realize his own true worth. You must give some time to your fellow man. Even if it's a little thing, do something for those who have need of man's help, something for which you get no pay but the privilege of using it.

> If you will devote your energies to innovation you must accept the following axioms:
>
> 1. You will never be liked or enthusiastically welcomed.
>
> 2. You will always be regarded with suspicion.
>
> 3. Your friends of today may be your hostile enemies of tomorrow. Your enemies of today may be your supporters tomorrow but *not for long.*
>
> 4. You will tread on people's toes. You can do this softly and maybe with some subtlety, but the pain will be there.

5. You are very much like a woman in the final stages of giving birth; you will not give birth without pain.

Robert W. Bradley
1323 Three Mile Drive
Grosse Pointe, MI 48230